12-1-94

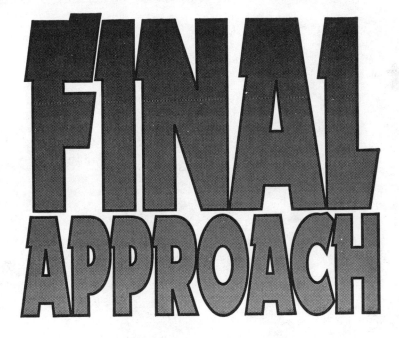

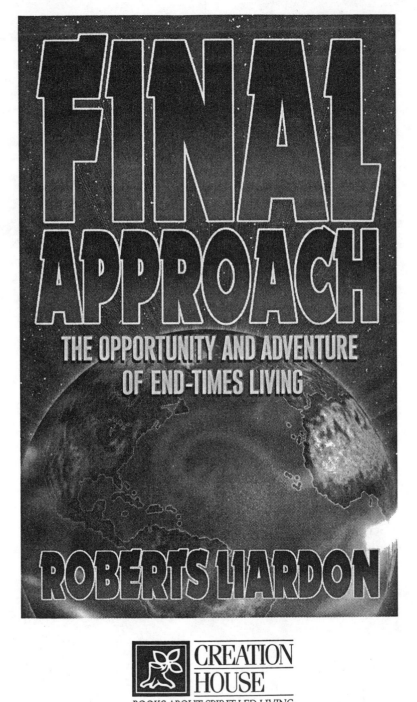

FINAL APPROACH

THE OPPORTUNITY AND ADVENTURE OF END-TIMES LIVING

ROBERTS LIARDON

CREATION
HOUSE
BOOKS ABOUT SPIRIT-LED LIVING
ORLANDO, FLORIDA

Creation House
Strang Communications Company
600 Rinehart Road
Lake Mary, FL 32746

CONTENTS

PREFACE

HAVE YOU ever been on a plane in a severe storm? It's a frightening experience. I can remember trips when I felt as if time after time the plane dropped hundreds of feet.

When it happens, everyone on the plane tries to look cool while feeling terrified, constantly looking around to see if anyone else is as worried as they are.

Actually very few passenger jets have crashed because of a midflight storm or air turbulence. By far the most dangerous and vulnerable times of the flight are the takeoff and landing. Any loss of power or concentration then can be disastrous.

The same is true for the church. At its "takeoff," Jesus baptized the small band of followers with His Holy Spirit and commissioned them to take the world. The Holy Spirit confirmed their message with demonstrations of power, helping them to spread the gospel successfully.

The apostle Paul testified before King Agrippa:

> For the king knoweth of these things, before whom also I speak freely: for I am persuaded that none of these things are hidden from him; for this thing was not done in a corner (Acts 26:26).

Notice what Paul said. These things were "not done in a corner." Paul and the other apostles weren't intimidated by anyone. They made sure everyone saw the power of God in demonstration.

Today, as the church makes its final approach toward its destiny, the power of God is just as vital. More than ever, people need to see God's power working in their lives. Many cults have sprung up and continue to grow because people everywhere long for the supernatural. The supernatural is built into every one of us because God created us, and He's supernatural.

Because some people haven't experienced God's supernatural power in operation, they've gone searching for it wherever they can find it. And the devil is more than happy to accommodate them with supernatural lies and deceptions.

All over the world, people are falling for the lies of the enemy because they are searching for their Creator God, whether they realize it or not. Inside every human being is that desire to know Him. The church exploded in the apostles' day because they showed people boldly who God was and what He was all about. Out in the open — not in a corner!

The Time of Conclusion

We are now living in the time of conclusion of all things. There's a general sense that the end is at hand. That's why we see so many save-this and save-that organizations. We have Save the Trees, Save the Whales, Save the Spotted Owls, Save the Planet groups all over the place. Even people in the world have enough sense to realize that time is ticking away.

Time *is* running out. But it has nothing to do with the natural order of things, although they will be affected. There is a spiritual reason for why things are happening the way they are. What's that reason? Jesus is coming back! We are standing at the threshold of the millennium. But we are not there *yet*. There's still some time left for us, and I believe we should make the most of it.

We have a great work to do for God. It is a work that cannot afford to be done in a corner. Like the apostles we shall see signs, wonders and miracles manifested through our lives — out in the open. People in this world must see the goodness of God, His healing power and His love for them.

How then shall we live in this time that is winding down? That's what this book is all about. It will show you how you can do the mighty works of God and live successfully and victoriously in these end days.

The people that do know their God shall

8

be strong, and do exploits (Dan. 11:32).

A Privileged Generation

We are living in the most thrilling, exciting time of the church. This generation is privileged to usher in our Lord and Savior, Jesus Christ. Sad to say, however, the way most Christians live is anything but thrilling or exciting.

Many Christians seem to have the attitude "Well, I'll just make it the best I can and rejoice when the rapture comes and we all get lifted out of this mess." Then some live in fear thinking, Oh, dear, what will I do when the Antichrist comes? Will I make it or not?

These should not be our attitudes at all!

There is so much confusion about the end times, the rapture of the church, the Antichrist and so on. One preacher will whip out all his fancy charts, Bible verses and proofs for a pre-tribulation rapture of the church. Then another preacher will come along right after him and argue for a post-tribulation rapture. Then others will convince you of multiple raptures before, during and after the tribulation.

Pre-trib, mid-trib, post-trib — on and on the debates go. Interestingly enough, those debates have been around for centuries. Do you know what my thinking is on this matter? Who cares! All those discussions and debates will just make your head spin.

It's not really important when the rapture will occur. What's important is what we are doing when it does. No matter what happens, we want Jesus to find us following His commmandments.

A friend of mine once told me, "I'm a 'pan-trib' believer."

That was a new one on me, so I asked, "What in the world is that?"

"I just believe that it will all pan out in the end," she replied.

Sometimes we get so caught up in the debates, arguing our positions and so on, we forget our real purpose for being here on planet Earth. Listen: if Jesus Christ is truly your Lord and Savior, you have nothing to worry about. It will most definitely all pan out in the end.

But until that end comes, we have a mighty work to do. That's what this book is all about — living in these end times and our responsibility in it. We are the generation concluding this dispensation. We should go out with a bang!

Life with Jesus is an ongoing adventure. Some Christians live dull, boring lives because they don't dare to live on the cutting edge. When you dare to do exactly what Jesus said to do, life is exciting and fun. That's the way it should be from now until the end, whenever and however it comes.

The Last Great Bachelor Party

In American culture there is a great whoop-de-do surrounding weddings. I am referring especially to the bachelor party. I've never been to one, but I sure have heard about them. Right before the groom gets married, all his buddies throw him a wild party. It's like the last great hurrah.

We are living in the days of the church's last great hurrah! We must make it count. Let's do everything we can to fulfill God's plans and purposes on the earth before we are joined to our Bridegroom. That is more important to me than when He comes. I know He's coming, but not even He knows when (Matt. 24:36).

If Jesus Himself doesn't know when, I figure I don't need to be wasting my time and energies trying to figure it all out either. The important thing to me is that when He does come, He will find me doing exactly what I'm supposed to be doing. I want to be ready for His return.

Jesus' parable of the ten virgins tells what will happen if we're not ready. Five of the girls were foolish, and five were wise (Matt. 25:2). The foolish ones didn't take oil for their lamps. Since the bridegroom was a long time in coming, they all became drowsy and fell asleep.

When the bridegroom came, the foolish virgins were not prepared to meet him. They were refused entry into the wedding banquet. They pounded on the door asking to be let in, and Jesus said that the bridegroom replied, "I tell you the truth, I don't know you" (Matt. 25:12, NIV).

Now Jesus didn't tell this parable to put the disciples into condemnation, fear and trembling. Instead He ended the parable by saying, "Therefore keep watch, because you do not know the day or the hour" (Matt. 25:13, NIV). The purpose of the parable was to exhort them to be about the Father's business up until the very last moment of time as we know it here on earth.

Next He told a parable about a man who went away on a long journey (Matt. 25:14-30). As the man was preparing to leave, he called his servants together and entrusted his property to them. He gave each servant different talents. After a long time, the master returned and settled accounts.

To two of the servants he said, "Well done, good and faithful servant." To the other he said, "You wicked, lazy servant." What was the difference between the three servants? Two did what he asked them to do; one did not.

Our Master has been away a long time, and He has entrusted this earth to us. When He does finally return, oh, that He would say of us, "Well done, good and faithful servants." I long to hear those words. Don't you?

I sincerely believe that this book will help you to live in your high calling in these times before us. It will help you to be a good, strong, bold witness in this final hour before His return. God will not receive honor and glory when His people are living in fear, worry or defeat. Instead, let us usher in His return boldly with victory.

1

WHAT TIME IS IT?

ISN'T IT exciting to be alive in these last days? Many times I walk into a meeting and ask that question. The response is almost always the same. People get happy, jump up and down, and scream and yell.

Excitement reigns in the meeting. But then everybody goes home, and it's a different story. Many people enjoy the high of a meeting, but they stress out at home where real life happens.

Why is that? Because some just do not know how to live in these last days. We listen to the radio or television news and read the morning paper, and everything looks bad. In fact, it looks downright depressing from a natural standpoint.

But we shouldn't be looking at things from a natural standpoint. The news media do not tell the whole story. We know God has a hand in the way things are going now. And He'll stay in control all the way to the end. That should make us happy, not sad, depressed or afraid.

We have a choice to make. Either we can live all stressed out and afraid in these end times that are before us, or we can enjoy them and have fun. That's right — *fun*.

Fun 'Til the End

Picture in your mind the following scene:

Two men, Jack Smith and Joe Brown, die and go to heaven. They're the same age and are born-again Christians. They arrive at the pearly gates together. As they walk through, a crowd comes running up. There standing before them are Noah, Abraham and Sarah, David and Jonathan, Ruth, Esther, Peter, Paul, John and Mary. In addition to all these greats from the Bible, other great leaders from church history are there with them — people like Martin Luther, John and Charles Wesley, John Knox, Maria Woodworth-Etter, Aimee Semple McPherson, Kathryn Kuhlman and many more.

All these great men and women come running up to Jack Smith and Joe Brown. Noah steps forward and says, "Tell us what's happening down there on earth. What has your life been like?"

"Yes, tell us," Abraham adds. "We've been waiting to hear all about it."

All the others murmur excitedly, "Yes, tell us — tell us."

14

Joe Brown clears his throat to say something, but Jack Smith cuts him off and starts in. "Well, you just wouldn't believe it. It is so horrible down there. The darkness is so strong. Sin is rampant. AIDS is killing people by the thousands. If that doesn't, abortion does.

"On top of that, drugs and crime are exploding everywhere. The occult, witchcraft and satanism are deceiving millions. Families are being torn apart. Two out of three marriages end in divorce, and most kids are being raised by either one parent or none.

"The planet is being destroyed. There are hardly any more dolphins, whales or forests. Then the Christians face all kinds of harassment and persecution from the media and the world. Our church split four or five times before I quit going.

"I tell you, it's been awful down there. I'm just glad to be up here with all you guys now. At least you have fun up here, don't you? It hasn't been any fun being down there on earth as a Christian in this day and age, I tell you. It's not anything like when you were alive."

Luther and the Wesley brothers almost speak in unison, "We faced harassment and persecution too, you know." Almost all the others nod in agreement.

"Well, yeah, I guess you did but not like we did," Jack says. "Why, we had these famous ministers who — "

Paul interrupts him. Turning to Joe, he asks, "What about you? How was it for you down there?"

"Well, what Jack said is true all right," Joe agrees, "but he didn't tell you the whole story. I, for one, was having a ball right up until the moment I ended up here."

"Now you're talking!" Peter exclaims. "You know all of us longed to live in your day. We saw your day and what it was going to be like, and we've all wished we could have lived in your time — "

"Peter, let the man talk," Mary interrupts gently.

Joe Brown continues, "Yes, we did see thousands die from AIDS, and millions of babies' lives were taken by abortion. But I also saw people totally delivered and healed from AIDS. And our church shut down the abortion clinics in our city. We also helped drug addicts get free."

"How did you do that?" David asks.

Joe looks at David and explains, "We learned some things from you about killing giants. We prayed, trusted God and got out there where the action was and did what we could. We cast out demons, healed the sick and changed things."

David nods and mutters, "Yeah, sounds like something I would have done." He turns to Jonathan, who is standing by his side.

"I like this guy," Jonathan whispers. "He sounds like one of us."

Joe Brown goes on to tell about all the people he introduced to Jesus; the missions trips he went on during his vacations; the miracles he saw when he visited his city's hospitals, nursing homes and prisons.

"What was it like in your church?" Ruth asks.

"We had a mighty move of God in our church," Joe says. "We started with about twenty people in Bible study and grew to three thousand that first year. Within five years just about everybody in our city was saved, and we had several churches of twenty thousand or more!"

Everybody starts cheering at this bit of news.

They keep asking Joe Brown more and more questions, and Jack Smith fades off into the crowd.

These two men were living in the same place at the same time. Yet they had two entirely different stories to tell. Jack's perspective was negative and fearful. Joe's was positive and bold. Joe was having fun in these end times. He was out there living life to the fullest up until the very end.

One man accomplished great exploits for God; the other didn't do much of anything except exist through life. Which man would you rather be associated with?

Unique Times Ahead

We are living in the most unique time in all of church history. I truly believe this is the church's finest hour. There has been no generation since that first generation of the church with such a unique responsibility as our generation has today.

The early Christians nurtured the baby church, which was birthed at Pentecost. Since then we have seen an infant church growing up into adolescence. Today we are living in the times that will see the church mature into the true bride of Christ.

Jesus said that the signs of the end of the age would be wars and rumors of wars, nations rising against each other and earthquakes. Then He said, "All these are the beginning of birth pains" (Matt. 24:8, NIV).

"We know that the whole creation has been groaning," Paul wrote, "as in the pains of childbirth right up to the present time" (Rom. 8:22, NIV).

The things we see going on in the world today

are the birth pains. As any woman who has borne children can tell you, those birth pains come at the crucial time of transition. The baby is getting ready to burst forth, and pain accompanies the miracle of birth.

We are living in a great time of change, a transition from one era to another. Christians must learn how to live and how to survive victoriously during this time of transition.

It's not just a question of mere survival either. We've got more to do than just exist until Jesus comes, gritting our teeth 'til the end. We are to claim and conquer new territories for God all over this world until that day comes.

Jesus told us to go into all the world with the gospel, make disciples of all nations, be bold witnesses everywhere — in Jerusalem, Judaea, Samaria and the uttermost part of the earth (Acts 1:8).

We are the final witness in this hour. That's our job description, and He's given us everything we need to get the job done.

Short-Circuiting God's Timing

Some Christians are short-circuiting. What do I mean by that? Simply that people don't know how to live in this transition time, this time of birth pains. The things they've always done and the way they've always ministered are not working as well, and they can't figure out why. So some people are pulling out of their callings; others are falling into the traps of Satan because they simply don't know how to live in this new era.

A pregnant woman will often go to special

classes to learn about the birth process and what to do and what not to do to make the experience easier on her and the baby.

In the same way, Christians need to learn how to live and move in God's perfect timing during this birthing time, this transition of the church.

As you see things changing in your life and ministry, don't mourn those things that God doesn't want you to do anymore. It's the same as growing older in the natural. You reach a point where you just don't keep on doing the same things.

As a kid you did all sorts of fun things. You really enjoyed doing them, and they worked for you. But as you grew up, the things you used to do with glee you no longer did — and you don't miss them. Every now and then, you might remember some things from your childhood with fondness, but you know those times are over.

That's exactly what has happened to the church today. It is growing out of one age into another and leaving the things of the past behind. Those who aren't willing to grow at the same time will miss the boat.

Throughout church history this has happened, so we shouldn't think it at all strange today. There have always been people who wanted to move on with God and go with the flow as He orchestrated it. But there have also always been those who bucked the change, or the different moves of God, so to speak. That's one reason why we have so many different denominations today.

Luther broke with the established church of his day and began what we know today as the Lutheran church. When you study history, you see that it was never Luther's idea to break away from the Catholic church. He wanted to stay in it, but they kicked him out and branded him a heretic.

Luther believed that we are saved by grace, through faith and not works (Eph. 2:8-9). In those days, proclaiming that the just shall live by faith was deemed heresy — but not today. That's because multitudes accepted Luther's ideas despite threats on their lives. They wanted to know the truth about God, no matter what the old, established group had to say about it.

Another great man from church history was John Wesley. When he originally broke with the established order, no one would allow him to preach in any church. The church world didn't like him. So he went to the fields and parks and preached. He preached life, and thousands were saved under his ministry. Out of that grew the Methodist church.

Get Out of the Rut

Many new denominations started because people grabbed hold of more of God. They wanted to keep going on with Him while others chose to stay in their old ruts. Sometimes people who won't change are afraid or just lazy. Change always means work, challenge and growth. And many don't like that. As a result, they miss out on what God is doing.

I don't know about you, but I want in on everything God is doing. But that doesn't mean easy street. Some people today find that they don't want to serve God as strongly as they once did because serving God today seems to be harder than it was ten years ago. It seems harder because it is harder!

Without understanding the anointing the Holy Spirit is pouring out, many people want to back off to an easier place to sit out the end times.

Christianity is not a spectator sport. We have no business just sitting it out until the rapture comes. We should be ashamed of ourselves if we ever think like that. Whether done from open rebellion, apathy or fear, sitting it out is sin.

God needs mighty warriors today, gladiators of His Spirit. He's looking for those who are willing to step into His arena and do battle to advance His purpose.

The main thing to understand is that times and seasons change in the Spirit, and we need to flow with them. If we get right in the midst of it all, it won't be so hard. But if we try to sit it out, direct it or resist it, it will be very difficult.

Spiritual and Natural Parallels

Christians who have lived through the turning points of history survived and got the victory by living in the Spirit. In times of great natural upheavals, equally great spiritual advances have often occurred.

The Pentecostal movement that turned the church world upside down was paralleled by World War I. The natural and spiritual worlds have never been the same.

A few years later, the church was fighting over who would be in charge of the airwaves. On one side were the modernists, liberal churches and liberal denominations. On the other side were the fundamentalists, evangelicals and Pentecostals.

You can look at television and listen to the radio

21

today and see that God's message of life won. Many of the people and ministers in the modernist movement were saved. But there were also many who were not willing to move out of their religious traditions and on into God's change of times and seasons. None of them is around today.

The healing revival was paralleled by World War II. Again, in both the spiritual and natural realms, this world has never been the same since. There were great shakings in both realms in the late thirties and on into the forties during that war. The healing revival began right at the time when World War II ended. It exploded onto the scene all over America and the world in the forties and fifties.

In the sixties another great shaking took place as the charismatic movement swept across denominations. The sixties and seventies saw a great harvest of souls, particularly within the hippie generation. It was a time of great rebellion in the natural world. Riots and demonstrations were commonplace. Vietnam and its issues caused chaos in our country, as well as in others. Yet a host of today's Christian leaders were saved in what has come to be known as the Jesus movement.

The point I am trying to make here is that you can see the parallels between the natural and spiritual realms throughout church history. Today it is the same.

There's a Whole Lot of Shaking Going On

Whenever God changes things in the spiritual realm, all that can be shaken is shaken (Heb. 12:26-27). The shaking produces the change He desires, and change is never easy.

22

Most of us don't like the reality of change. We like to live in an imaginary world where we all live happily ever after. But the only place faith works is when we are dealing with reality. Faith changes the world's reality to God's reality. God's reality is always good, so we shouldn't ever be afraid of it or the changes it brings.

Some Christians are trying to live as if they were already in the millennium. Yes, the Lord is coming back. Yes, the millennium is coming. But we are not there yet.

The church must do many things before the millennium arrives. We must spread the gospel worldwide and reach many souls for Jesus before the time they speak of comes.

This gospel of the kingdom will be preached in the whole world as a testimony to all nations, and then the end will come (Matt. 24:14, NIV).

On the other side of the fence you have those who are afraid of everything and want to stick their heads in the sand like ostriches and escape from this world. Neither attitude accomplishes much of anything for God's kingdom.

I grew up as a Pentecostal. When I was a little boy it seemed we were always focused on the fear side of the end-times passages. After hearing about the tribulation and the Antichrist, we'd all run around declaring that we'd never take the mark of the beast. We were petrified of the guillotine that prophecy teachers thought was going to be restored to use. We watched a movie about the end times, and it scared us for weeks.

The Bible tells us it is God's kindness — not fear — that leads men to repentance (Rom. 2:4, NIV). But Jesus' teaching to His disciples in Matthew 24 was always cast in a bad light.

Jesus never intended for His people to run around like chickens being chased for Sunday dinner. He did not ask us to focus on the negative, even though the negative will be there. Jesus simply said, "Take heed that no man deceive you" (Matt. 24:4).

Discernment for Good, Not Just for Evil

Jesus instructed His disciples to "take heed." He was telling them to be discerning. He didn't expect them to be overtaken with fear. Some in the church today seem to operate in a cloud of paranoia. They are so afraid of being deceived that it has opened the door to deception itself. What you fear most will often come upon you, as Christians should have learned from Job's experience (Job 3:25).

Deception is like a magnet. Your paranoia of deception attracts deceit to you — if only by causing you to fall into an opposite extreme of what you fear. Instead of being deceived by others, you are deceiving yourself.

The gift of discernment is like a spiritual antenna. To live victoriously in the last days, our receivers need to be fine-tuned. We need discernment to recognize the thing God is doing, as well as the counterfeits. When people talk about discerning of spirits, they seem to imply that devils are everywhere. It is even more important to discern the presence of the Holy Spirit and of angels.

Spiritual discernment does not cause you to

snoop into people's lives and ministries that are none of your business. If you need to know something about someone else, the Spirit Himself will show you so you can help that person. We don't need any more spiritual spies and snoops going around destroying others' lives and ministries.

Having been raised in Pentecostal circles, I have seen many people do things just because someone else did them that way. That doesn't take any spiritual discernment whatsoever. And just because they worked for someone else doesn't mean they will work for you.

The early Pentecostals did some things that looked strange to many, but they were done under a divine unction with a divine purpose. However, as their children, grandchildren and great-grandchildren grew up, they saw those actions and imitated them. That is called tradition, and tradition nullifies the Word of God (Matt. 15:6).

How do you develop discernment in your life? The best way is to pray in the Spirit. This builds up your spiritual sensitivity. Praying in the Spirit means foregoing some things your flesh may like.

Remember, though, as you are praying in the Spirit and developing sensitivity to His voice, not everything you discern is to be talked about or brought out into the open. Sometimes all you are to do is pray about something the Spirit reveals to you.

Flakes and Weirdos

In these days to come, we will see every kind of "weirdo" and "flake" imaginable involved in the things of God. But just because some people go offtrack, we don't have an excuse for throwing out what God is doing. We need to discern the things of God and realize there will always be people who miss the mark or who misuse His revelations, whether for healing or deliverance or prosperity.

What is your point of reference — the flake or the Word? Mine is the Word!

Just because I fly through Tokyo on my return to the United States from Asia does not mean that I become Japanese. Some people will operate in particular gifts of the Holy Spirit and then turn the wrong way. Just because they get off into error does not mean that you have to do the same. Just because you traveled through the same territory on your route with the Lord does not make you a flake.

We've got to keep in mind, however, that new does not automatically mean flaky. Ministries are coming into the world today that the church at large does not even know about. They are out in the wilderness of preparation as Moses was. The Holy Spirit is training them, and they will come forth with great zeal.

When these new ministries burst forth, we should not cast suspicion on them because they don't do things the same way as in the past. We need to see them according to the Spirit and not the flesh. We must be discerning in these last days so we don't miss out on what God is doing.

Divine Approval

Jesus was aware of the spiritual timing of events in His walk here on earth. "My time is not yet come," He said (John 7:6). Then, "when the time was come that he should be received up, he sted-fastly set his face to go to Jerusalem" (Luke 9:51).

Jesus never moved out of God's timing and season for Him. He did not allow other men to move Him either. Some wanted to make Him king, but Jesus resisted them. Sadly, the approval of men has caused trouble for many Christians. In studying the lives of many past leaders, I discovered that when the applause of men grew great, those leaders thought that meant approval from God.

Divine approval does not come from the hands of men. You can feel it in your heart and spirit when God's approval is upon you, no matter what people may say or do. Public opinion is often misguided.

Be Not Troubled

Jesus said, "Ye shall hear of wars and rumours of wars: see that ye *be not troubled*: for all these things must come to pass, but the end is not yet" (Matt. 24:6, italics added).

In the natural those are troubling words. But Jesus said these things must come to pass. So when they do we should rejoice because it simply means that we are getting closer to the end. It does not take six months to decide not to be troubled. Decide in your heart right now by faith not to be troubled.

Jesus made another statement when talking about all the horrible things to come: "The end is not yet" (Matt. 24:6). We are at the beginning of the end, but the end is not yet. Let's heed Jesus' advice and not be troubled. End-times living means opportunity and adventure.

Look at what has recently been happening in

27

Eastern Europe, for example. The Berlin Wall came crashing down, and the Soviet Union came apart at the seams. It took everybody by surprise. Mikhail Gorbachev got a lot of the credit. He even won the Nobel Peace Prize in 1990. But make no mistake about it: man did not bring about these things. God did, and it didn't take Him by surprise.

When those things started happening, people kept asking me, "What do you think about all this? What does it all mean in light of end-times prophecy?"

What people wanted was an analysis to satisfy their intellectual reasoning or curiosity. Many wanted to know which hidden verse in Ezekiel or Daniel or Revelation explained it all. People were looking for some deep, secret prophecy to be fulfilled.

Well, my answer to all their questions shocked them. "The big revelation about the Berlin Wall is this: we can go in and out.

"It means it's time to take advantage of it. It's time to go in behind those old walls and save souls, heal the sick and get people delivered and launched out into their callings so they can fulfill God's plan and purposes on this earth."

That is the significant thing about all the happenings in Eastern Europe. The kingdom of God can declare itself among those nations that have been closed for so many years. Matthew 24:14 can now be fulfilled in that part of the world.

And this gospel of the kingdom shall be preached in all the world for a witness unto all nations; and then shall the end come (Matt. 24:14).

28

Instead of spending a lot of time and energy trying to analyze every world crisis and make it fit into end-times prophecy, we need to see all these things as God's doors of opportunity. Now is the time to go and preach the gospel that is supposed to be taken to the world before the end comes.

That's exactly what is happening in Eastern Europe now. There has been a major influx of missionaries and ministers into that area from other countries. Many of God's people worldwide have jumped at the opportunities to go in and plunder hell in those places. As a result, thousands of people are being saved, and the church is growing and being strengthened.

When end-times events occur, they will always open a door of opportunity. We are not called just to sit back in our nice American homes, lolling about in our hot tubs, vegetating in front of the boob tube, trying to decipher the news. *The believer must see world events as divine opportunities to do the work of the gospel.*

Everyone in the church should be out doing something for God.

A True Hero of Faith

I recently heard of a young man who went on a missions trip to India. Now India is not the easiest country to go to. A lot of ministers would never dream of going there because it's so tough spiritually and physically. But this young man decided to go and do what he could for the Lord in that tough land. That in itself may not sound unusual; some Christians go there often to preach. But this man was unique in that he had muscular dystrophy.

29

He and the team he was with would be walking down the street and all of a sudden they would notice he wasn't walking with them anymore. They would look back and see him collapsed in the dust because the muscles in his legs had given out. So they'd pick him up and carry him until strength came back into his body. He had to be carried up and down stairs, but he never complained.

He counted it a privilege to take the gospel to India. He could have sat at home having a pity party over his physical condition. Instead, he rose up believing God for healing, and while waiting for the healing to manifest he dared to go where most will never go with the gospel.

I like hearing stories about people like that. They are the true heroes of faith. In spite of everything that has come against him, that young man chose to be out taking Jesus where He was not known.

All of us have that choice to make. End-times living means taking your vacation out on the mission field. Think on eternal things. Even if you never have before, now is the time to be thinking, Eternity is at stake. Take whatever opportunity there is to participate in the adventure of preaching the gospel to the nations.

You may be saying, But I can't go to the mission field. There are some legitimate reasons why some people cannot go to a foreign field. But even America has become a mission field. Thousands of people are living right here in our own country, sitting in unbelievable darkness.

This country is no longer the place of God it used to be. Noted Christian scholars call this the post-Christian era in America. I am not saying that to be negative; I wish it weren't true. But it is the truth. I daresay that there are people living right on the same street as you who are headed to hell, without having heard about the love of Jesus. If we truly love Jesus, we will love to tell others about Him.

For some that may mean a real sacrifice. It may mean leaving your home and those nice comfort zones and getting out on the front lines of world harvest.

We Win the Race by Running, Not by Sitting or Discussing

Get rid of every weight and sin that so easily entangles you so that you can run well the race before you (Heb. 12:1, NIV). Only you and God know what those weights are. Get honest with Him, and He'll help deliver you from them.

This is our finest hour, church. Do you remember when Britain was at war in World War II? Winston Churchill, the leader of their nation, stood up and declared boldly, "This is our finest hour."

I'm sure there were plenty of people who thought differently. They were in the midst of war. Many of their cities had been destroyed by bombs. People were living in shelters under the street. Yet he proclaimed, "This is our finest hour." Those words became a rallying point for the people. Somehow those words spoken by Churchill brought about the change that was needed.

Today this world is at war on every side. The forces of evil are out to destroy mankind in every hideous way possible. But where sin abounds, grace abounds much more (Rom. 5:20).

31

Yes, there are great challenges ahead of us. Yet, according to the Bible, these end-times days will be the church's finest hour. God's Word has decreed it — it shall come to pass.

The church is to be a glorious church — not a church full of fear and frustration, waiting to be rescued out of this mess. Warnings about end times don't have to make us paranoid. We can go into these end times rejoicing. Even in the midst of troubled times and battles, we can look forward with joy to the end.

2

JOY: A POTENT FORCE

JOY IS a force that knocks cares from you, a force that knocks despair off you and a force that helps you walk through every tribulation and persecution with victory. Joy is absolutely essential for life in these end times. With joy, living in this final hour can be an adventure. Without it we are not going to be effective witnesses.

Many Christians today just don't have as much joy operating in their lives and ministries as they need. After they leave a church service, finish listening to an anointed tape or close an inspiring book, their joy disappears. That's not true spiritual joy.

Isaiah 61:3 says that Jesus will anoint us with the oil of joy and give us garments of praise. He will give us new spiritual clothing. Our garments of praise will chase away the spirit of heaviness.

In the natural it's not always easy to break forth into praise when things aren't all fine, but you can do it. Make the choice to be joyful.

Habakkuk 3:17-18 says:

Although the fig tree shall not blossom, neither shall fruit be in the vines; the labour of the olive shall fail, and the fields shall yield no meat; the flock shall be cut off from the fold, and there shall be no herd in the stalls: yet I will rejoice in the Lord, I will joy in the God of my salvation.

Habakkuk tells us that we can possess joy even in the midst of hard times and battles.

You can enjoy yourself in whatever battle of faith you're fighting. For we know that greater is He who is in us than he who is in the world (1 John 4:4). Beating up on the devil should be fun.

James 1:2-3 says that we're to count it all joy when we encounter hard times. How can you be joyful in the middle of the trials and tribulations that life has to offer? You can be joyful because you know God will give you the victory.

Joy will give you the strength you need to fight every battle to the finish and win. The Bible says that the joy of the Lord is our strength (Neh. 8:10). Do we really believe that? If so, then we must keep our joy level up.

There are some verses in Psalm 51 that I particularly like.

Create in me a clean heart, O God; and renew a right spirit within me. Cast me not away from thy presence; and take not thy holy spirit from me. Restore unto me the joy of thy salvation; and uphold me with thy free spirit (Ps. 51:10-12).

We do not need a new baptism of joy. We simply need to return to the joy we once had. That joy is the joy of our salvation, the joy of being born again and washed in the blood of Jesus. It's the joy of knowing that our names are written in the Book of Life.

How to Keep Your Joy

It is a fight to keep that precious joy of your salvation. But remember: if the devil can't steal your joy, he can't steal your goods. Don't let the devil steal your joy in any way, shape or form.

Just because some other sour-faced, depressed Christian doesn't have any joy operating in his life doesn't mean you have to live that way, too.

So how do you keep your joy? You keep it by choosing to be joyful even when you don't feel like it — most especially when you don't feel like it. Joy is not a feeling. Joy is a state of being.

You can be joyful by faith. Choose to believe God rather than what your mind is trying to tell you or what your soulish feelings are screaming. Remember: you are a spirit; you have a soul; you live in a body. Pull down vain imaginations, and keep yourself immersed in the Word.

Whatsover things are true, whatsoever

things are honest, whatsoever things are just, whatsoever things are pure, whatsoever things are lovely, whatsoever things are of good report; if there be any virtue, and if there be any praise, think on these things (Phil. 4:8).

This is a vital key to keeping your joy level up. When a bad report comes, refuse to dwell upon it. God's Word says to think on the good report. Change your thinking so you can walk in joy.

In these final days there will be plenty of bad reports unleashed against God's people. Joy will put you over them.

Have Fun With God

We always seem to be seeking God with heaviness of heart. At times you will have great burdens and serious questions in prayer. You can go to the Lord and cast your cares upon Him (1 Pet. 5:7). When you do that, He will give you an answer.

However, there should also be times when you inquire of God with joy. Some people do not know how to inquire of heaven in this way. They do not know that you can bounce right up to the Father, jump in His lap and say, "I've come to have some fun."

One facet of God's character is fun. Religion makes God seem heavy, serious and solemn all the time. But think about this: each of us has a sense of humor to one degree or another. Isn't that true? And remember that we were created in the image of God. So humor must be a part of God's character.

If humor is a part of God's character, then it

must be good. If you have a sense of humor, a desire for fun and joy, then rejoice. You had to get it from your Father because every good and perfect gift comes to us from the Father (James 1:17).

In the Bible you can see God's sense of humor from beginning to end. God likes to have fun. What about the time when God told Gideon's army to surround the enemy and then break empty jars and blow trumpets. They looked ridiculous, but the enemy screamed and turned on each other (Judg. 7:20-22). Or what about that little shepherd boy who killed the giant? The same little boy who later became king? Don't tell me that God doesn't have a sense of humor. He's got the best humor of all time.

God gave us a sense of humor so we could enjoy life. He didn't put us here to live a miserable existence. However, God's joy is vastly different from worldly joy. The world's joy is based on circumstances. From the world's perspective, when things are going well, people feel happy. But then when things are in a tumult and a shaking is going on, they become sad. There is no permanency in their happiness because it is always based on external circumstances.

True Christian joy is nothing like the world's joy. Christian joy is being joyful and happy regardless of the circumstances — whether they are good, bad or indifferent. In His presence is fullness of joy (Ps. 16:11).

Some Christians never experience real joy — never walk continually in joy — because they don't spend time in His presence. The more time you spend with Him, the more joyful you will become. You will begin to see things the way He sees them.

Joy Is God's Medicine

In Proverbs 17:22 a merry heart is referred to as a medicine. To have a merry heart is to be full of joy. Joy is a spiritual "drug," a medicine for the ills of the soul.

Just as there are natural medicines that make you immune to certain diseases, so joy is a spiritual medicine that will make you immune to the cares of this life.

Joy helps you through that period of waiting — the period between the time you prayed and the time the answer to your prayer manifests. Without joy it's a long, dreary time of waiting. But with joy we can wait with faith and patience. It is through faith and patience that we inherit the promises (Heb. 6:12).

Choose Joy

James makes it clear that joy is a choice.

My brethren, count it all joy when ye fall into divers temptations; knowing this, that the trying of your faith worketh patience (James 1:2-3).

James was not writing to the world in general here. He said, "My brethren." He was writing to believers in Christ. He did not tell them to run from temptation but to be joyous — "count it all joy" — when you have a chance to use your faith against temptation.

Many people give up instead of facing struggles head-on so they can overcome them. They try to go under their problems, around them or over them instead of blasting through them. Without joy everything seems strenuous.

Joy puts things in proper perspective. In our natural human nature, problems often seem so big. Joy will help you see the answer.

Joy is a force of protection as well as a force of happiness. We must transmit joy to one another and to the world. That's the only way we are going to overcome in this day of conflict, wars and other fulfillments of end-times prophecies.

Escaping Worry

In every temptation God makes a way of escape (1 Cor. 10:13). I believe the way of escape from the temptations of worry, fretting and stress is to be joyful. Learn to be amused instead of depressed. That will keep your joy manifesting.

When things seem sad or doubtful, learn to see what is happy or funny in them. Make the choice to be joyful no matter what. Even when you are happy, choose to be more joyful.

Laughter of the Soul

We've talked about the great difference between the joy of the Lord and the "joy" of the world. We often associate joy with laughter, but there is a laughter of the soul that is not real joy. This ranges from the malicious, evil laughter of those walking in satanic influence to snickering, rude laughter, crude remarks or dirty jokes. Most Christians would never be guilty of these counterfeits of God's joy.

There is also carnal (soulish) laughter that is not demonic or crude; yet it is not of God. I was in a church once with a pastor who seemed very nice. I was able to spend a lot of personal time with him. I liked him, but he was always laughing and doing silly things.

He cracked jokes and played tricks all the time. It was not the fun of the Spirit, nor was it fellowship fun. It was carnal and fleshly. He did not curse nor tell rude jokes, but his laughter was not right.

This attitude affected his ministry. Several people tried to help him deal with it, but he would say, "Oh, I just like to have a good time." Time after time he shrugged off their concern. Eventually he caused a church split over his carnal attitude.

We all want to have a good time, but if you allow yourself to get involved in coarse jesting and foolish talk all the time, it will destroy the sensitivity of your spirit. You will miss those things God is trying to speak to your heart. So be careful. You can find the balance by watching whether or not your heart is at peace. Follow after peace, and you can't go wrong.

Joy Robbers

There are robbers of joy just as there are robbers of faith, peace and boldness. If you want to be strong in the Lord, you must keep your joy.

Robber 1: Rooted in the Natural

Being rooted in this earthly life is one big joy robber. This life here on earth is temporary. The Bible says that we have an inheritance reserved in heaven (Heb. 11:9). Sometimes there are too many cords binding us to earthly functions and cares. We need to unhook from the earthly cares, the cares of this life, and hook up to heaven, our real home (Col. 3:1-2).

Jesus warned that the cares of this life weigh down the heart and keep us from being ready for His return (Luke 21:34). In the parable of the sower Jesus warned that the cares of this life keep a Christian from producing the fruits of righteousness (Mark 4:3-9). Without joy from His presence this world and its cares will rob you from producing anything of lasting value.

Robber 2: Not Knowing How to Live in Tough Times

Yes, there will be tough times. Welcome to life. Many Christians have been taught that if tough times come, something must be wrong with their faith. That is not the case most of the time.

Often the hard times come from your opponent. The enemy comes to harass, hinder and challenge you. We are not exempt from trials and hard times just because we are people of faith.

Look at the apostle Paul. He was one of the greatest men of faith the church world has probably ever seen. Yet he was left for dead more than once, beaten, shipwrecked, robbed — you name it and Paul faced it. Yet he kept on praising God. He didn't think it at all unusual to encounter tough times. Neither did he view them as marks against one's spirituality. In fact, he indicated that it was an honor to be persecuted.

> Beloved, think it not strange concerning the fiery trial which is to try you, as

though some strange thing happened unto you: but rejoice, inasmuch as ye are partakers of Christ's sufferings; that, when his glory shall be revealed, ye may be glad also with exceeding joy (1 Pet. 4:12-13).

In these end days before us, there will be tough times. The devil knows that his time is growing short, and he's not about to go out without putting up a fight. We need to be prepared to face the battles. Don't let those battles rob you of your strength — your joy!

Robber 3: Pickiness

Pickiness also robs people of their joy. Some people let anything — no matter how insignificant — upset them. They become petty little people, criticizing anyone who tries to do anything.

"I don't like the way the pastor laughs," they say. "I don't like that song leader's hair." "The parking situation at that church drives me nuts." They eventually leave the church and sometimes leave the Lord because of their self-centered, judgmental attitudes.

I've heard almost every excuse people give for nursing a bad attitude. What difference does it make how someone combs his hair or what his speech patterns are like? None of that matters in the long run. Don't let pickiness steal the excitement and joy away from your heart.

Robber 4: The Flesh

Joy will help you keep your commitment to God's work fun when your flesh is telling you, "This is no fun." For example, I travel a lot, and my flesh gets tired of airplanes, hotel rooms, rude waitresses and smoky restaurants.

I have a nice apartment and a good bed at home. Sometimes when I'm on the road, I just want to go back to my own home, sleep in my own bed for a change and eat the food I like to eat.

Now my flesh could scream at me all the time, but I don't let it. I tell it to shut up. Then I make myself rejoice wherever I am at the moment — whether it's on a straw mat in some village, a pull-out couch in some pastor's study or a fancy hotel suite. Choosing to joy in these things makes my commitment to my call and ministry fun.

Traveling may sound like fun for those who don't do it much. Many traveling salesmen have reached the place where they give up six-figure incomes because they don't like the travel. Traveling is just like anything else. It gets old very fast.

Whatever you have to deal with — traveling or not traveling, too much to do or too little to do — joy in life begins with the decision to deny the flesh and choose to rejoice. I choose to stay heavenly minded in those situations and keep my thoughts on good things (Phil. 4:8).

The pull of the flesh and the pull of the world become strong on a person who has no joy. He feels like quitting on God. Worldly, fleshly desires can seem like more fun than the spiritual fun we can have in God. The flesh will try to take over spiritual desires. But joy is the balancing force.

If you set your affections only on your career, money, material possessions, worldly philosophies and knowledge, they will possess you and consume your life. If you set your affections on the things of heaven, your spirit and mind will be built up and enriched.

The pull of the world and the flesh will get stronger in these last days. You have to be strong in the joy of the Lord to withstand those pulls.

Robber 5: Demonic Acts Against You

When Paul and Silas were in Philippi, they were continually followed and harassed by a slave girl who was possessed by a spirit of divination. Finally, Paul got fed up and cast out the devil in the name of Jesus (Acts 16:16-24). You would have thought everybody in town would be thrilled that the girl had been delivered. Instead, these two great servants of God were stripped of their clothes, beaten with "many stripes" and thrown in prison.

All of that happened because the girl's masters lost their fortune-telling business when Paul cast out her spirit of divination. These men stirred up a mob and accused Paul and Silas falsely of creating a civil disturbance and preaching things against the state.

You have not been beaten with whips for your faith, but you may have been beaten up in the spirit with people's words, actions, rejections and frustrations.

We can learn from Paul and Silas's example. As they were sitting in their prison cell, they prayed and sang praises to God. If they could keep their joy when their backs were bleeding, surely we can do the same — even if our hearts are bleeding.

Paul and Silas sang loud enough for all the other prisoners to hear them (Acts 16:25). They were fervent in their singing and praising. If you are not fervent, you will not be able to overcome the devil and your flesh when those hard times hit.

Fervent prayers and fervent singing bring your head and body into agreement with your spirit. You see, your spirit knows the right thing to do. That's why David told himself, "Bless the Lord, O my soul" (Ps. 103:1).

Encouraging Yourself in the Lord

David knew if he was to maintain his joy, he had to encourage himself in the Lord. You see, joy comes from inside you. It's up to us to draw it out.

It's a lot like priming a pump. Before it was common for people to have running water, most homes had a hand pump that drew water to the surface and into a bucket. To get a pump going, you have to prime it. You put a small amount of water into the pump, start working the lever, and before you know it the water begins to flow. There may be an ocean of water at the bottom of that well, but you'll die of thirst if you don't know how to prime the pump.

Jesus said that if we drink of the water He gives, it will become a well of water springing up to eternal life. The joy of the Lord is like well water. You've got to prime the pump to get it flowing. As we encourage ourselves, it primes that joy deep inside us to rise up and flow forth. When you learn to bless the Lord and sing and praise Him in the hard situations of life, God will shake the prison doors and loose the bands that hold you. Joy that flows from the Spirit of God is an empowering and delivering force.

We won't need to prime the pump of joy when we're in heaven. It's here on earth that we get to do

45

this. As you encourage yourself, that joy will bubble up and become stronger and stronger.

If you are joyful, people's words and actions against you won't seem as powerful. The devil doesn't seem as strong when the joy of the Lord is your strength. In the midst of criticism and persecution, you can be happy and irritate the devil to no end. Now that's *fun*.

You can have fun in the middle of a problem as you watch the Holy Spirit work it out for you. Joy shows you a whole different side of the Trinity. When you are joyful and happy in trials, it attracts God to you because you are acting on your faith. The apostle Paul said:

> For the kingdom of God is not meat and drink; but righteousness, and peace, and *joy* in the Holy Ghost (Rom. 14:17, italics added).

The side of us that has fun is like Him. He gave us fun and laughter when He made us so we could enjoy life. Joy is also contagious. We can give it to one another.

Some people think that being a Christian means you always have to be serious. That is not going to attract people to you or to God. Demons love for you to be serious all of the time — the wrong kind of serious. But Christian joy irritates the devil. If he cannot get you concerned, upset, sad or depressed, he cannot have any fun. Right now, make up your mind to spoil the devil's fun from now on.

Remember — joy is a choice. When you encounter a tough time, you face a crossroad: the street of sadness, seriousness and wrong *or* the count-it-all-joy path. You make a choice for joy or sadness every time. You will find that it is just as easy to choose joy once you make up your mind to get in agreement with the Holy Spirit and not the devil.

Joy is also "oil" in a marriage or a friendship. Like the oil in an engine, joy keeps everything going right. Paul wrote to the Philippians that he did "joy" and "rejoice" with them (Phil. 2:17). I feel this way about some churches in which I've preached. I can hardly wait to go back to see them again. Where there is a spirit of joy, we have great services.

Kathryn Kuhlman once said of a minister, "I like him because he makes me laugh." That is what we ought to be able to say about our friends.

Break Forth Into Joy

Look at Isaiah 52:9.

> Break forth into joy, sing together, ye waste places of Jerusalem: for the Lord hath comforted his people, he hath redeemed Jerusalem.

The prophet again shows that breaking forth into joy is a choice. Choose to break forth with joy and singing. Keep breaking forth. Do not let your flesh get heavy and sit down on you. One way I can tell if someone is living in the Spirit is if that person has joy. You always have joy when you walk in the Spirit rather than in the flesh.

It is not always easy to have joy, to laugh and be hilarious. But break forth into joy, and it will become easy. There is nothing wrong with clean Christian laughter.

Don't allow others to make you feel ashamed of being joyful and happy. Some Christians are so religious that they think you have to be downhearted and solemn all the time. They confuse seriousness with spirituality. This happened to me when I started in the ministry. People told me over and over, "You need to be more serious, Roberts. You make it look too easy, too fun."

You can have fun doing the works of Jesus. We can have a lot of fun and joy in our church services. It helps people see that the church isn't full of a bunch of deadbeats.

Joy Meets the Need

Joy helps heal a hurting heart. People come into churches with hurts and needs. If they don't find any happiness and joy, they'll never get the spiritual help they need.

I look at my generation and think, No wonder some of them don't want to go to church. There is no joy in churches. There is no fun! If people aren't happy about being a child of God, there is not much there to attract people to Jesus.

Smack dab in the middle of God, there is *fun*. Oh, yes, there are times of seriousness, times of guidance and warnings from God. But there should also be times of rejoicing, shouting, dancing and singing before the Lord without restraint.

You can laugh your way out of hurt as well as pray your way out. We need to be open to this method of healing and answered prayer. You can laugh and cry at the same time, but when you are finished, you will be free.

Earlier I quoted this prayer of King David:

48

Restore unto me the joy of thy salvation; and uphold me with thy free spirit. Then will I teach transgressors thy ways; and sinners shall be converted unto thee (Ps. 51:12-13).

King David knew that leading transgressors and sinners into the way of the Lord required joy on his part. I enjoy the ministry. I am having fun serving Jesus. You can have fun, too.

The kind of fun that is godly comes from a joyful heart. Spiritual fun does not mean you ignore serious issues. It simply means that you know spiritual things can also be joyous. You know that worldly things aren't worth getting upset about.

Even when circumstances look tough, joy causes you to understand that you already have the victory — and that calls for rejoicing.

Those of us who are alive in these end times are going to find life challenging, exciting and fun.

3

ENDURANCE
FINISHES
THE RACE

A RUNNER GETS a second wind — a burst of
strength — as he rounds the last lap of his
race and heads for the finish line.

God is giving us a second wind during the final
laps before the end. It's an added burst of strength,
a special anointing to enable us to *endure* all the
way to the final moment.

That little word *endure* used to bug me. It almost
made me cringe on the inside whenever I heard it.
It seemed like such a hard word that meant basically to suffer and grit your teeth until this is all
over. Or else it meant we would be beaten into the
ground, barely making it — and then the rapture

would come. If we just somehow endured, then we would be raptured out.

Now I know better. *Endure* is a good word, a blessed word. It means "courage and strength to see you through." End-times responsibility is more than just waiting around, gritting your teeth until the rapture happens. When Jesus snatches us away, we will not be hiding out, babbling, "Oh, praise God, now we're out of all that mess. I didn't think I could stand it another minute."

Absolutely not! I believe the end-times church will say, "Give us more time for the gospel's sake. Lord, just a few more days, weeks, months or years. More souls are at stake. I just want one more soul, Lord."

In military terms *endurance* means "to hold up courageously under fire." It does not mean "The bullets are flying, but I'm hanging on." That's called "scared under fire." Jesus said that he who endures to the end shall be saved (Matt. 24:13). Spiritual endurance is not wearing yourself out; it is continuing on with courage from the Holy Spirit.

Holy Boldness Always Endures Successfully

One time when Paul and Silas were in jail, they praised God so loudly that everyone else heard them. Strength and courage came through their prayers and praise. They weren't covering their faces in shame, whispering, "O God, if it be Thy will, get us out of here!" No, they sang forth God's praises loudly.

Doubt has a weak voice, but faith has an amplifier built into it. Paul and Silas did not get upset and squall about their miserable situation or try to

51

figure out how to get out of jail. They endured with faith, strength, courage and *boldness.*

Great opportunity requires great boldness. That is why the Spirit is calling the people of God to a greater aggressiveness and intensity. Carnal Christians will back away from the spiritual intensity required in the days just before us. They won't be able to handle the intense preaching, prayer and worship of these last days.

Carnal Christians will resist the word of the Lord that is coming because it doesn't fit into their religious traditions. We can't play church any longer. The religious way of functioning will be blasted, not by those who are going on with God, but simply by the times in which we live. It will be hard on people who want to stay lukewarm.

> I know thy works, that thou art neither cold nor hot: I would thou wert cold or hot. So then because thou art lukewarm, and neither cold nor hot, I will spue thee out of my mouth (Rev. 3:15-16).

That word *spue* literally means "vomit." It's a gruesome picture. No Christian in his right mind would want to be vomited from God's mouth.

Second Thessalonians 2:3 mentions a "falling away" that will occur when some Christians refuse to let go of the natural things of life that entangle them. They won't go over into the realm of the Spirit and live as the early church once did.

We need to get back to the way of the disciples and the early church, letting the nature of the Spirit dominate our activities. The disciples were totally sold out and committed to the gospel, no matter what happened. They were dead to self and alive to Jesus. As John said, "He must increase, but I must decrease" (John 3:30).

Jesus warned that the love of many would "wax cold" (Matt. 24:12). Some worn-out, stressed-out, burned-out Christians are in this category today. Once in this state, they just sit back and exist through life. But those who refuse to wax cold will endure to the end.

Endure What?

Enduring spiritually means to hold up courageously under fire — under affliction. The apostle Paul endured some hard things — persecution, beatings, prison, shipwreck and robberies. Yet he called them "light affliction" (2 Cor. 4:17).

Light affliction! If that's light, I wonder what hard affliction would mean to him. Paul found that enduring affliction produces tremendous joy (Phil. 2:17-18). Joy will help us endure any affliction — light or hard. When affliction comes, don't be offended, betrayed or hurt. Get that joy going. It causes a heavy affliction to be light.

Running Instructions

There is a race set before us in these times.

Wherefore seeing we also are compassed about with so great a cloud of witnesses, let us lay aside every weight, and the sin which doth so easily beset us, and let us run with patience the race that is set before us (Heb. 12:1).

We are to fulfill our duty and finish the race. In that verse the writer of Hebrews gives the following instructions:

1. *Lay aside every weight, and lay aside sin.*

It is not always the obvious weights or the obvious sins that keep you from finishing the race. When we speak of sin, some Christians think of carnal sins — eating too much, drinking, doing drugs, watching too much television, committing adultery, stealing, coveting or murder. But it is usually the sneaky sins, the things we think of as minor, that are the real hindrances in our lives. Sometimes we need Holy Spirit revelation even to see that we have these sins.

One sin might be the lack of diligence in spiritual things. That is a sin, you know. Set your affections on the things above and not on the things of the world (Col. 3:2).

2. *Run the race set before you with patience.*

If we are going to finish the race of the last days, we cannot be sprinters — those who have great endurance for only a short distance. We must settle down to a steady, patient, ground-covering pace. No matter how fast the pace of the outer world seems to be, we must run by the pace of the inward witness.

> And not only so, but we glory in tribulations also: knowing that tribulation worketh *patience* (Rom. 5:3, italics added).

> And let us not be weary in well doing: for in due season we shall reap, if we faint not (Gal. 6:9).

For ye have need of *patience*, that, after ye have done the will of God, ye might receive the promise (Heb. 10:36, italics added).

And beside this, giving all diligence, add to your faith virtue; and to virtue knowledge; and to knowledge temperance; and to temperance *patience*; and to patience godliness (2 Pet. 1:5-6, italics added).

Fixed on Jesus

In a natural race the runner keeps his mind and body focused on that finish line as he rounds the last lap. He doesn't trot haphazardly along, gazing up at the sky or looking for someone in the bleachers. No, he is completely focused on the finish line in front of him. He runs the race to win.

To endure to the end, we must also keep our eyes fixed on the finish line where Jesus is waiting for us with the crown of life.

Looking unto Jesus the author and finisher of our faith; who for the joy that was set before him endured the cross, despising the shame, and is set down at the right hand of the throne of God (Heb. 12:2).

There will be some people in this time who simply won't realize that it is the end time. They will continue to live casually and carnally as if it didn't really matter. They won't have the spiritual stamina to finish the race. There will also be people who fight the final activity of the church out of ignorance, jealousy or fear. They can be very distracting, but we can't use up our energy by focusing on these people.

Other people will let their focus slip onto the circumstances of life or the negative things around them. When you stop looking at Him and look down at the waves around you, you will sink as Peter did (Matt. 14:30).

A few years ago many Christians were distracted by books proclaiming the rapture at a specified time. People were deceived by this false teaching, and it caused the church to be a laughing stock in the world's view. People were actually ringing up all kinds of bad debts, figuring they would be gone shortly anyway. That's a horrible witness to the world.

When that happened, I asked the Lord about those books. Those who believed that teaching had a real expectancy in their souls that the rapture was at hand. It grieved me. I couldn't figure out how they were so deceived. The Lord told me that the people were filled with fear. They had no patience and no purpose on earth and just wanted to leave and get it all over with.

It's normal that we would be happy to go to be with Jesus for all of eternity. Every Christian looks forward to that with expectancy. That's not wrong. But these people allowed their ears to be tickled by false teaching because of their desire to leave this earth. They didn't want to take the responsibility of staying here and doing what Jesus said to do. They did not want to develop faith and strength of spiritual character through dealing with and enduring the tests and trials of everyday life. They got distracted and decided to quit running the race.

When you have no purpose for being here, you

have no reason to stay. The only purpose the church has been taught is just to get out of this place. The majority of Christians don't believe the end times have much to do with them. But the end times have everything to do with us. And it's not just to escape trouble.

Trouble Is Normal

Christians in China, Nepal and the former Soviet Union have had much trouble, tribulation and persecution in this century. Imprisonment, torture and death for being a Christian have been occurring in those places for a long time. It's almost normal for them.

From the days of the early church we have been warned that trouble — or tribulation — is the "normal" situation for Christians.

These things I have spoken unto you, that in me ye might have peace. In the world ye shall have *tribulation*: but be of good cheer; I have overcome the world (John 16:33, italics added).

...confirming the souls of the disciples, and exhorting them to continue in the faith, and that we must through much *tribulation* enter into the kingdom of God (Acts 14:22, italics added).

We are strangers to this world's system, cultures and ideas. The god of this world order is not our God (2 Cor. 4:4). That is why we have tribulation on this earth. But our God reigns over all creation.

Jesus is not coming back for a scared, "wimpy" bride, whipped by tribulation. He is coming for a strong bride — the glorious church. When the Lord comes, He is going to find a happy bride, one without spot or wrinkle (Eph. 5:27).

The minute spiritual warfare or persecution begins, some Christians say, "Well, if that's the way it is here, I'm going somewhere else."

I like what John Osteen said about his church:

A lot of people think they helped build this church. But they were not here in the beginning hours when we began to walk around the walls of Jericho. They came on the last round when everyone was yelling excitedly, and the warfare had already been done. They just came for the party. They didn't do any work.

To endure *tribulation* means you have joy, patience and peace of mind. It means you work at what your hands find to do. The party will come later.

Endure for the Harvest

America has a spiritual role in the end times — to enlist, train and launch Christians into all nations of the world to preach the gospel.

God will use those who endure patiently to bring in a great harvest during these last days.

Be patient therefore, brethren, unto the coming of the Lord. Behold, the husbandman waiteth for the precious fruit of the earth, and hath long patience for it, until he receive the early and latter rain (James 5:7).

Right now the former Soviet Union and Eastern Europe are more open to the gospel than they have been in more than forty years. Communism is dead, pulled down in part because of the prayers of the saints.

Some people think the walls will go back up, and the Soviet Union will begin another cold war. If that happens, it will be very hard to fool the people in those nations again. They have had a taste of freedom and a glimpse of the truth.

For years people in the Baltic states were told they had a better life than their neighbors, the Scandinavian countries. They believed people in Scandinavia were starving and oppressed under a capitalist system. When the borders opened, people from the Baltic states filled their suitcases with canned goods to take as they visited their starving cousins in Scandinavia. But upon arrival they found things were exactly the opposite of what they had been told.

Seventy years of deception have gone down the drain. People there are hungry for the truth we have to give them. America's main job is to preach the gospel to every creature throughout the world through television, radio, personal preaching, printed materials, books, financial support, prayer and any other avenue that God opens to us.

Let the politicians play the games, but let the believers run the race!

The Power of Prayer

In order to endure spiritually, hold up coura-geously under fire and run the race with patience and joy, you *must* pray. Strong prayer puts courage into your heart.

Your time of praying in the Spirit should in-crease in these last days. The church is beginning to gain more understanding about the dynamics of praying in tongues. Exercising this gift builds a sensitivity to the moving of the Holy Spirit. The more you pray in tongues, the stronger you will become in your inner man.

Prayers from a prophetic anointing will also come forth — not only from individuals, but corpo-rately. In the last days, all of us — the entire church — will pray in unity.

Corporate Influence

Several years ago some ministers began to prophesy about "corporate" anointing and opera-tions of God. I was there when these first prophe-cies came forth. I did not understand all of them, but I knew in my spirit that this was truth. I grabbed hold of that word and said, "I believe."

When you know from an inner witness that something is from God, grab hold of it even if you do not understand all of it. I still do not understand everything about corporate anointings and the cor-porate flow of the Spirit.

At the time my mind translated corporate to be about twenty-five people. But I have found from God that corporate may mean twenty-five thou-sand people. It will take that many people to change cities and open nations. God is going to move whole nations to prayer. The prayer that goes forth on national prayer days will rock the nations of the world. Demons will not know what hit them because they have forgotten how strongly Christians can pray. Principalities and powers that have been left alone for hundreds of years are going to come up against a force that will not back down.

Enduring Influence

One day as I drove around sightseeing in a city I had never visited before, I saw many beautiful church buildings. In the spirit I started to see a kind of ring or circle showing the extent of each church's influence. Some churches only had a ring of influence that went out two or three blocks from the building. The Lord said, "They have grown happy with their little space. They like their two blocks of influence and want to leave the rest for someone else." Other churches had no circle of influence at all. All they had was a building!

In these end times, a two-block influence will not do. The influence that counts for eternity will reach all nations. It takes strong prayer to maintain that influence.

Praise and Worship Endurance

Praise and worship are another part of spiritual endurance. Get rid of the spirit of heaviness and put on the garment of praise. Don't settle for nice, quiet, little services that do not disturb any person — much less any demonic force that may be in the vicinity.

Strong praise coming forth out of our spirits will break the power of the heavens and bring a fresh anointing. Praise and worship services will shake the atmospheres of cities in greater dimensions than we have ever imagined. We need to be ready for them.

There is no limit to God's strength and power. It is from everlasting to everlasting. We can tap into it and soar with it, allowing the might of God to come on earth through our worship and praise. Then we shall see His glory.

The Purpose of His Glory

The heavens declare the glory of God; and skies proclaim the work of his hands. Day after day they pour forth speech; night after night they display knowledge (Ps. 19:1-2, NIV).

God's glory does not come for a show but to demonstrate His reality. In these days He is causing men to preach His glory again, just as the heavens show forth His glory. He has called some to put together large prayer armies or to teach prayer. He has brought a new anointing on those praise and worship leaders who will receive it.

There is coming revelation knowledge of the glory of the Lord. We must hold on to the purpose of His glory. Doing so will keep us on track and bring us to the finish line.

Arise, shine; for thy light is come, and the glory of the Lord is risen upon thee. For, behold, the darkness shall cover the earth, and gross darkness the people: but the Lord shall arise upon thee, and his glory shall be seen upon thee (Is. 60:1-2).

When will His glory be upon you? Isaiah said it would be when "gross darkness" covers the earth. At the time of great darkness, God's glory shines through. For example, when the plague of darkness fell on Egypt, the Israelites were basking in light. God's glory is on those who obey Him and endure to the end.

This is not a sad day for the church; it is a triumphant day. Where sin and darkness abound, grace does much more abound (Rom. 5:20).

You may be thinking, But I thought that we would not have to go through the tough end times. Let's face it: we are already in tough times. Just read the newspapers and watch the television news; they say, "Welcome to end times and hardships." We are in the last days of the last days. Don't think you'll be gone before the hard times come.

Know this: great harvesting will happen as hard times come. The enemy will try harder than in all previous centuries to stop, abort or delay the harvest, but he won't be able to do it.

A bold, aggressive intensity is being born into the people of God today to enable us to fulfill end-times responsibility. Tough times call for tough Christians — genuine, strong warriors of God who will endure.

4

WE ARE
IN WAR

EVERY PERIOD of church history has experienced spiritual warfare, but it will intensify in these last days. As the end draws closer, the devil will pull out all the stops. Be ready for it. Spiritual warfare is a reality for the church in this day.

The Bible mentions the theme of war many times, even describing our Lord as a warrior!

The Lord is a warrior — yes, Jehovah is his name (Ex. 15:3, TLB).

The first spiritual battle that ever took place was in heaven.

And there was war in heaven: Michael and his angels fought against the dragon; and the dragon fought and his angels, and prevailed not; neither was their place found any more in heaven (Rev. 12:7-8).

Michael and his angels were created for battle. They didn't come against Lucifer with fluttering wings on fluffy clouds of glory. No, they fought. And they won.

Notice — they *won*. That's important. We should always go into warfare determined to win. Otherwise we're defeated before the battle begins. We don't want a spiritual Vietnam on our hands. Because the military entered that war without a clear command to win, they could never claim a victory.

Contrast the outcome of Vietnam with the decisive victory we saw in the Gulf War in 1991. What was the difference? The military was sent into the Gulf War with a totally different attitude. General Norman Schwarzkopf refused to begin like Vietnam. They began with a winning attitude that said, "We shall win. We'll do whatever it takes and will not leave until we win."

How different from the Vietnam War which was labeled a police action. No one asserted boldly, "We are declaring war on you. Our goal is to overtake and stop you, destroy your ideas and bring ours in."

We must enter spiritual warfare with a determination to fight until the finish and to *win*. Some who say they oppose the devil and his destruction in people's lives don't really want to wage warfare. I call them "public relations warriors." They talk the talk, but in the battle they won't walk the walk. So the enemy just keeps gaining more and more ground.

I refuse to be just a public relations soldier. I want to get in there and win. In these last days before us, we must be ready for warfare. The devil must be stopped. We have a clear-cut command to win.

Winning Warfare

For years, the church has been satisfied with a police state — protecting what she's got. It reminds me of the people of Israel wandering in the desert during the days of Moses. They experienced the supernatural: Their clothes never wore out, there was not a sick or feeble person among them, and food was miraculously provided to them every day. We're talking about a big crowd to feed, too!

Though a degree of the supernatural was operating, they never pushed ahead with it. They kept going around in circles in their own little world. They left Egypt, but they didn't get rid of the spirit of Egypt. They just maintained and policed what they had until a new generation rose up — a generation of faith and action that knew how to advance in war, attack and do battle.

When there are battles to be fought, God always prepares a generation of warriors.

> Here is a list of the nations the Lord left in the land to test the new generation of Israel who had not experienced the wars of Canaan.
> For God wanted to give opportunity to the youth of Israel to exercise faith and

obedience in conquering their enemies (Judg. 3:1-2, TLB).

The King James Version says that God left them there "to teach them to war." God wants His people to be skilled in war. Even if people live in a time of peace, they're always ready for battle if they are skilled in war.

Many think it's a time of peace today, but it's not. The church is battling right now for the nations of this world. From now until the end there will be no peace. If God warned His people in the Old Testament to stay skilled in war, how much more serious it is to learn the spiritual art of war today. This generation must be skilled at war so that God can fulfill His plans and purposes for this hour.

A successful warfare is one where you *win*. Michael fought the angels of Lucifer in heaven and kicked them out. He won the first war ever to take place. The second war took place in the Garden of Eden over a man's will. The outcome of that war would determine who controlled the destiny of man and creation. It looked as if the devil won that battle, but he really didn't. The war didn't end until Jesus battled the devil — and won!

Today we're here to fulfill Jesus' victory.

Soldiers of Christ

Thou therefore endure hardness, as a good soldier of Jesus Christ. No man that warreth entangleth himself with the affairs of this life; that he may please him who hath chosen him to be a soldier (2 Tim. 2:3-4).

67

The Lord chose us to be His soldiers. This is not a volunteer army; every Christian has been drafted. There are no conscientious objectors in His army. We are soldiers, and that's all there is to it.

Matthew 11:12 tells us:

And from the days of John the Baptist until now *the kingdom of heaven suffereth violence, and the violent take it by force* (italics added).

The body of Christ must use a degree of spiritual aggression to continue gaining ground in the nations. Yet we do not fight against people in the physical realm. Our fight is in the spirit.

For we wrestle not against flesh and blood, but against principalities, against powers, against the rulers of the darkness of this world, against spiritual wickedness in high places (Eph. 6:12).

Spiritual violence has nothing to do with physical violence or abuse. Spiritual warfare is simply coming against the spiritual darkness of this world.

Jesus came against spiritual darkness. The Bible says the reason He came was to destroy the works of the enemy (1 John 3:8). The Bible also says we are like Jesus in this world (1 John 4:17).

It is so important to understand that we are to destroy the devil's works. Christianity is not just a little bless-me club where we all go to get happy.

God raises up warriors to fight in the battles He

ordains. For example, He appointed the Medes to execute His judgment on the Babylonians. God said, "Thou art my battle axe and weapons of war" (Jer. 51:20). God created us to be warriors for battle up until the very end.

The Great Command

When Jesus gave us the Great Commission, He commanded us to destroy the works of the enemy. It might be better to call it the Great Command. "Go ye into all the world," Jesus said (Mark 16:15). Unfortunately, many people interpret that to mean "Stay here and wait for the world to come to you."

That command *to go* is a command of invasion, advancement and attack. He said to invade the world with His love and power, telling every creature the good news. That doesn't mean we only go to those who like us or approve of what we do. We also go to those who sit in darkness — the Moslems, Hindus and Buddhists of the world — and set them free.

How do we set people free from darkness? Let's look at what Jesus told the disciples after He gave them the Great Commission.

And these signs shall follow them that believe; In my name shall they cast out devils; they shall speak with new tongues; they shall take up serpents; and if they drink any deadly thing, it shall not hurt them; they shall lay hands on the sick, and they shall recover (Mark 16:16-18).

First He said they would cast out devils. Then

He said they would pray in tongues. He went from one wild thing to the next telling the disciples, "You *shall* do it." He didn't suggest, "If you feel like it, maybe you'll consider using signs as a testimony of My power." He said the signs would "follow them."

Jesus has given us the same power to set people free from darkness. And He's commanded *every one* of us to go and conquer in His name. We're to advance and attack the enemy's territory, taking back ground that he stole from us.

The Soldier's Job Description

If we are soldiers and warriors — and we are — then that means we have a job to do. Paul gave us our job description in 2 Corinthians 10:3-5.

> It is true that I am an ordinary, weak human being, but I don't use human plans and methods to win my battles. I use God's mighty weapons, not those made by men, to knock down the devil's strongholds.
>
> These weapons can break down every proud argument against God and every wall that can be built to keep men from finding him. With these weapons I can capture rebels and bring them back to God, and change them into men whose hearts' desire is obedience to Christ (TLB).

No earthly army would go off to war without the proper weapons and equipment. God also makes sure His army has everything it needs to wage warfare. Paul describes some of our weapons, too.

Wherefore take unto you the whole armor of God, that ye may be able to withstand in the evil day, and having done all, to stand. Stand therefore, having your loins girt about with truth, and having on the breastplate of righteousness; and your feet shod with the preparation of the gospel of peace; above all, taking the shield of faith, wherewith ye shall be able to quench all the fiery darts of the wicked.
And take the helmet of salvation, and the sword of the Spirit, which is the word of God: praying always with all prayer and supplication in the Spirit, and watching thereunto with all perseverance and supplication for all saints (Eph. 6:13-18).

Paul very clearly tells us what our weapons are and what to do with them.

With Spirit Power

In addition to these powerful weapons God has given us something else to help us wage a successful warfare. It's something that Jesus had.

God anointed Jesus of Nazareth with the Holy Ghost and with power (Acts 10:38).

Jesus went about doing good and healing all who were oppressed of the devil because He had the power of the Holy Spirit.
Every true soldier must be anointed with the Holy Spirit's power. You can't fight the devil and his oppressive ways with natural human might.

71

You'll get beat up every time if you do. You fight spiritual darkness with God's weapons in the power of the Holy Spirit. God placed a fighter inside every one of us.

I have a missionary friend who was attacked by a robber. She was walking down a busy city street when a man shoved her, punched her and started banging her head against a wall. He was trying to get her purse. She didn't just stand there saying, "Oh, I see — you are going to injure me and take my purse. Don't let me stop you." She put up a fight.

That's what we're to do — fight. That's what a soldier is trained to do — fight. Some of God's soldiers are afraid to fight, so they're always getting beat up. Listen: it's fun to get in the midst of a spiritual battle because you know you will *win*.

The Lion Within You

The devil is walking about like a lion, seeking whom he may devour (1 Pet. 5:8). Notice that the verse says he is "like" a lion (NIV). The devil is not *the* lion; he just pretends to be one. Jesus is the lion living in you with His might and power. But you must know it and act upon it to be a good soldier of war.

I learned this several years ago on one of my very first trips to Africa. One day we ran smack dab into the middle of a war. We were driving along a bumpy dirt road when chaos erupted. Our truck slammed on its brakes, and we all jumped out. As I stood in the middle of the road, I felt as though bugs were whizzing by my ears. Then I realized they were bullets — real bullets. We all lunged for the ditch next to the road.

We huddled down in the ditch to shield our bodies from the bullets as the grass around us was crushed by machine gun fire. I did not feel any precious anointing as I lay in that ditch. Nor did I hear angel's wings. I did not receive some magnificent vision of the Lord coming in all His power and might. I didn't even have a song to sing. All I could do was quote Bible verses nonstop and pray. I prayed as I never had before.

I know the Lord heard my prayers, but I did not feel any protection or safety. I felt like a totally naked person out in the middle of a battleground. I told my angels, "Listen, you guys — if I die, you're going to get it! So you better not leave me today."

I wouldn't have known what to do with a gun if someone had handed me one. I may have found the trigger, but I wouldn't have known how to reload it. I was not prepared at all. I was not trained in the use of weapons. I didn't have the proper experience or knowledge.

Just as I was unprepared in that natural battle, some Christians are unprepared for a spiritual battle and have no idea what to do. They hide in the ditch, terrified and totally unprepared. In the very early hours of the conflicts to come, they'll realize that the buzzing in their ears is not the sound of fuzzy, little bugs. It's the sound of the real bullets and bombs of the enemy.

The enemy's attacks are designed to destroy what God is doing in the nations through His church. We don't have to hide in fear because God has equipped us with all the weapons we need to win every battle of the end times. But as Hosea 4:6 tells us, people can be destroyed for lack of knowledge.

73

Unprepared Christians may wind up like some of the people I saw when that fight in Africa was over. Many people were seriously injured or lost their lives that day. Bodies were lying in the brush. It was not a pretty picture. Unprepared Christians may literally lose their lives in the warfare of these end times. Others will wax cold because of the events of the times.

Mao Tse-tung, past leader of China, once said, "Armament is an important factor in war but not the decisive factor. Man, not material, forms the decisive factor." In other words, it's not the weapons that determine the outcome of a war — it's the people who carry them.

The same can be said about spiritual warfare. God has given us all the weapons we need. Do we know how to use them? He's trying to impart to His people the discipline, revelation, anointing and ability to be successful end-times warriors.

Spiritual warfare is not a trend; it's knowledge to endure happily and successfully in this time before us. The Spirit wants to get His people prepared because the times demand it. Operating in spiritual warfare must be a part of us. If not, what are you going to do when the bombs go off next to you? Are you going to know how to get through it? Are the last days going to be exciting for you, or sad?

If you will hear what the Lord is saying to His people in these end times, you can rise to the occasion and be an integral part of the church's finest hour.

Trained for Battle

I have learned a few things about spiritual warfare that I believe will help prepare and train you for battle. One necessary thing is a haven of peace where you can hear the Holy Spirit without interference, a place without the enemy's influence. This will keep you strong and charged up.

I like going to my home where the atmosphere is clean. I don't let the garbage from television, the radio and so forth contaminate it. I can rest in the peace and liberty there and pray without distractions. Since I am on the road so much, I need to rest when I come home.

It is also essential that I keep my home free of the ungodly influences others might possibly bring in with them. Some people let ungodly influences in and then battle to get them out again. It's a whole lot easier to keep influences out if you never let them in. Keep your home free and peaceful so you can rest and pray effectively.

When I travel, I encounter all kinds of warfare that I never face at home. Some of my greatest battles occur in hotel rooms because of all the things that took place in that room before I got there. I have no control over who was there and what went on before I got there.

In addition to your home, if you are in ministry, you need to keep your offices free from ungodly influences. Both your home and your ministry offices need to have a strong, clean environment. This kind of environment will keep you strong and rested up so that you can wage a good fight successfully in the spiritual realm.

Intensified Warfare

As we get closer to the coming of the Lord, spiritual warfare is going to intensify. We are not called to fight a minor battle. We fight major battles.

Paul told the Corinthians that he fought with "beasts" at Ephesus (1 Cor. 15:32). Is he talking about natural beasts like lions and tigers and bears? No, he was referring to spiritual beasts — principalities and powers over Ephesus. In Ephesus the principality was a demonic strongman masquerading as, or calling itself, "the goddess Diana."

The book of Acts describes Paul's encounter at Ephesus. Paul taught at Ephesus for more than two years, healing the sick and casting out demons. Many of the people had practiced sorcery, but because of Paul's ministry they renounced those evil practices.

It was to the Ephesians that Paul wrote these words:

> For we wrestle not against flesh and blood, but against principalities, against powers, against the rulers of the darkness of this world, against spiritual wickedness in high places (Eph. 6:12).

When Paul entered a city or town, he went straight for the main "evil prince" over that place. Paul was outspoken in his warfare. When you are going after principalities, you must be bold. It does no good to beat around the bush when you are dealing with spiritual powers. Listen to how the followers of Diana at Ephesus complained about Paul.

> Moreover ye see and hear, that not alone at Ephesus, but almost throughout all Asia, this Paul hath persuaded and turned away much people, saying that they be no gods, which are made with hands.
>
> So that not only this our craft is in danger to be set at nought; but also that the temple of the great goddess Diana should be despised, and her magnificence should be destroyed, whom all Asia and the world worshippeth (Acts 19:26-27).

The leaders in Ephesus stirred up the people against Paul, kidnapped two of his traveling companions and started a riot. What was Paul's reaction? He wanted to go and talk to them, but the disciples restrained him (Acts 19:30). Paul loved to fight principalities. He loved to preach sermons that provoked and alarmed the powers that be — the principalities over a place. He didn't back down when they began to get stirred up. His attitude was "Let me go in there and preach some more. Let me at them."

You must be bold and outspoken like Paul when you are going after principalities. It does no good to beat around the bush when you are dealing with spiritual powers. Stay in the battle until you accomplish what God wants and you have the victory.

Acts 19:32 describes what finally happened to the group of Ephesians who were opposing Paul.

> Some therefore cried one thing, and some another: for the assembly was confused; and the more part knew not wherefore they were come together.

Paul's blow against that principality was so hard that it sent the people into confusion. Confusion disables the enemy.

Paul advanced boldly against the principalities that were trying to hinder God's work. That same ability is in every Christian. We are all called to bring righteousness to this world of darkness. This is our end-times duty to the nations of the world.

Spiritual Warfare in Prayer

One way that we can wage a successful battle in the spirit realm is through prayer. For the classic biblical example of spiritual warfare through prayer, let's look at Daniel 10:12-14.

> Fear not, Daniel: for from the first day that thou didst set thine heart to understand, and to chasten thyself before thy God, thy words were heard, and I am come for thy words.
>
> But the prince of the kingdom of Persia withstood me one and twenty days: but, lo, Michael, one of the chief princes, came to help me; and I remained there with the kings of Persia.
>
> Now I am come to make thee understand what shall befall thy people in the latter days: for yet the vision is for many days.

Notice that a response was released from heaven as soon as Daniel began to pray. But in the realm of the spirit, the angel with the answer was delayed by the evil prince of Persia. War ensued in the heavenlies as Michael came to the aid of the embattled angel.

More of the angelic host than we have ever been aware of will help us as we fight spiritual battles over nations. Warrior angels are assigned to help us fight territorial wars. But though angels are fighting on our behalf, we cannot stop doing what we know to do. We must continue to pray and fast, just as Daniel did. The messenger angel went right back into the war zone when he left Daniel (Dan. 10:20).

Believers today have one important advantage over Daniel: Jesus has defeated Satan once and for all at Calvary. In Daniel's day Satan had not yet been defeated. Today we are just fighting cleanup skirmishes and guerilla warfare against those enemies still hidden in *our* territories.

We can always chase out the enemy in Jesus' name. There is no spiritual battle you cannot win — but you have to fight. John Wesley once said that he did not believe God would do anything unless somebody prayed. If we will be strong, bold warriors in prayer, we will see God do great things on our behalf and on behalf of the nations.

Spiritual Warfare in Prophecy

Another weapon in spiritual warfare is prophecy, the word of the Lord coming forth through one of His ambassadors. For example, the prophet Ezekiel was called to prophesy against the prince of Tyrus.

The word of the Lord came again unto me, saying, Son of man, say unto the prince of

Tyrus, Thus saith the Lord God; Because thine heart is lifted up, and thou hast said, I am a God, I sit in the seat of God, in the midst of the seas; yet thou art a man, and not God, though thou set thine heart as the heart of God (Ezek. 28:1-2).

The prince of Tyrus had apparently been taken over totally by Satan. In fact, later in the chapter Ezekiel calls Satan the "king" of Tyrus, an obvious link to the "prince" of Tyrus. Satan's original calling and his career as a fallen heavenly being are also spelled out (Ezek. 28:12-17). God had called Ezekiel to speak out against Satan, prophesying his horrible end (Ezek. 28:18-19).

Paul wrote to Timothy about the prophetic call on his life.

This charge I commit unto thee, son Timothy, according to the prophecies which went before on thee, that thou by them mightest war a good warfare (1 Tim. 1:18).

Notice that Paul told Timothy to engage in good warfare *by the prophecies* that Timothy had received. To warfare by prophecy you must hear what God has said and hold to it. You speak it out in the name of Jesus so that the rulers of the darkness in that place must hear it and obey.

When you do this, you can expect warfare to intensify. Learn to believe and stand on those words of God so that they can come to pass in the earth.

Changing Spiritual Climates

When principalities are bound, cultures change. This happened during the Welsh Revival in 1906. Coal miners, prostitutes and all kinds of rough people flocked to the churches and got saved. Many of the saloons were turned into chapels. Even the ponies had to change. That was because the ponies hauling carts of coal out of the coal mines had been commanded by curse words. When the miners quit cursing, they had to teach the ponies new commands — or get new ponies. As people drove down the road in horse-drawn buggies, the power of God would fall on them. They would stop, fall to the ground and lie there a couple of hours. Then they would get saved.

These things happened because the heavens were broken open, principalities were bound, and the glory of God came down. The principalities over Wales had been pulled down through prayer, praise and worship — not through great preaching and teaching.

Our calling in this hour is to change the spiritual climate of cities and nations. Evil spiritual influences pervert people's views of Jesus. In some places people think of Jesus in such weird ways. Those thoughts come from the evil powers sitting over their city, throwing out lies and vain imaginings. Spiritual warfare can break down those influences.

At times governments get upset at the church when they sense an authority knocking down those evil rulers in their cities. But they cannot figure it out because it is a spiritual thing. They just know that they feel uneasy, threatened and frightened.

Usually, those feelings are not their own — the feelings come from the demonic powers over the city. People would realize this if they understood the spirit realm.

After I preached about spiritual warfare recently, a lady let me know my message didn't exactly thrill her. "I guess I have to do this warfare stuff," she said, "but I really don't want to. I don't enjoy it, even though I know deep in my heart that you are right. I'll be glad when the Lord just comes and takes us out of this, so that we can live in heaven and be nice and peaceful."

As she spoke, the Holy Spirit said to me, "Doesn't she know that we're all coming back for one great battle after that?" People who do not like to think about warfare do not understand that it is going to go on even after the rapture.

We also need to know that you can be a nice person and still be a mighty warrior. Somehow people have the idea that if you are a great warrior, you are mean. A mighty warrior is not mean but powerful. He is strong and accurate in the Spirit.

I once watched a film that was supposed to show the history of the early church. I got upset and turned it off when I saw it depicting Paul, Peter and other early Christians running through the streets at night, hiding in fear. Obviously they hadn't read the book of Acts where it says they went publicly into city squares. They walked boldly into the synagogues and preached against tradition. They prophesied and provoked those who carried demonic influence and the demonic powers over regions. That's our calling, too.

Summary

Spiritual warfare expresses the love of God in a powerful way. You will not change your city or nation through social programs or nice little sermons and nice prayers.

Be aware that people — as well as demonic forces — will come against you in spiritual warfare. Many people are in alignment — consciously or unconsciously — with the princes over their cities. They will fight against you and your church or ministry in the natural. Remember that your fight is not against flesh and blood. You battle the demons behind them. But if you persevere, endure in a good fight of faith and pull down those supernatural forces, God can turn what is going on in the natural to your benefit.

Strong love that desires to see change in people's lives won't quit when the going gets tough. Wars with principalities or strongmen do not happen overnight so don't ask when it's going to end. Just keep invading and possessing until the victory is won.

God is using His people — His warriors — to change nations today and to build a divine base from which He can launch His mighty warriors into other enemy territory. The army of the Lord is marching on!

5

SERVING AN EXTRAORDINARY GOD

SEVERAL YEARS ago I was in Pittsburgh, Pennsylvania, doing some research on a book about Kathryn Kuhlman. As I visited church people who had lived in that area all their lives, I'd ask them, "Did you go to any of Kathryn's Bible studies?"

Their answers astounded me. One person actually said, "No, I didn't think they were worth going to."

God was moving mightily through one of His servants, one of the greatest miracle workers of the day, in the place where these people lived. Yet they didn't feel they needed to be at the meetings.

There's something wrong with a lazy, complacent attitude like that. Thousands of people traveled from all over the world to get into one of Kathryn's meetings, and yet Christians right there in the same city said, "No big deal."

They had let God become too commonplace. Their hearts had grown cold to the things of God because they didn't esteem Him highly as they should. They missed out totally on what God was doing in their time because they had a ho-hum attitude toward the things of God.

The best way to make sure God never becomes commonplace in your life is to keep that first love alive. Keep that initial excitement about Jesus burning strong, always looking for what God will do.

Some people sit at home watching soap operas or sitcoms while God performs miracles right across town in a meeting. They miss out. If you keep your spiritual eyes and ears tuned in, you'll know when God is doing something. You can't run around to every meeting — but don't miss out on the ones where God is working.

People from all over the world attended the Azusa Street revival in Los Angeles in 1906. The crude building where they met had been a livery stable at one time. That's not the first time God used a stable to initiate something major in His plan. God is not commonplace, but His presence transforms the commonplace.

God doesn't do things the way we would imagine they should be done. If it had been up to us, His Son would probably have been born in a luxurious royal palace. Instead God chose a place where animals slept. A meeting in a not-so-flashy building does not mean it's unimportant. Don't be moved by the outward trappings. Be inside where God is moving.

God's choice of Tulsa as a central spiritual hub may seem odd. It's not situated in the midst of beautiful scenery like Colorado or San Francisco. Tulsa is not even easy to get to. You have to fly through Chicago, Dallas, Denver or St. Louis to visit it. It's really a very ordinary, nondescript kind of place in the middle of nowhere. Yet God chose it and made it extraordinary.

Some of the greatest Pentecostal preachers of all time prophesied about Tulsa's future. Some of my friends in Tulsa have told me how God began speaking through His preachers in the early 1900s when the place had barely become a state, sitting out in the middle of Indian Territory. He said, "I'm going to bless Tulsa. I have a future for this place."

That future began to manifest thirty or forty years ago. Yet today there are still people living in Tulsa who don't have the foggiest idea what God is doing. He's become too commonplace to many. Don't let God become commonplace in your life.

Watching From Afar Off

When you serve an extraordinary God, you're going to miss out if you just stand off in the distance and watch. Let's look at how Elisha and the prophets reacted when Elijah was taken up to heaven (see 2 Kin. 2:1-18).

There were schools of ministry in Bethel and Jericho during Elijah's time, whose students were called "the sons of the prophets" (2 Kin. 2:3). They knew in their spirits that Elijah would be taken to heaven; they asked Elisha if *he* knew his master was going to be taken that day (2 Kin. 2:3). However, only Elisha had the courage, endurance and desire to make sure he was close at hand when God moved.

> And Elijah said unto Elisha, Tarry here, I pray thee; for the Lord hath sent me to Bethel. And Elisha said unto him, As the Lord liveth, and as thy soul liveth, I will not leave thee. So they went down to Bethel.
> And Elijah said unto him, Elisha, tarry here, I pray thee; for the Lord hath sent me to Jericho. And he said, As the Lord liveth, and as thy soul liveth, I will not leave thee. So they came to Jericho.
> And Elijah said unto him, Tarry, I pray thee, here; for the Lord hath sent me to Jordan. And he said, As the Lord liveth, I will not leave thee. And they two went on (2 Kin. 2:2,4,6).

When the sons of the prophets asked Elisha if he knew what was happening, he basically said, "Yes, I know, but don't bother me. I'm on a divine mission. I am here to get something."

The sons of the prophets were satisfied to know that something was happening. They just sat back and watched and didn't get in on it. They should have said to Elisha, "If you follow Elijah, then we'll follow you. We want some of that anointing you are getting today. We want our part."

Fifty prophets watched from a distance as Elijah and Elisha stood by the Jordan. Elijah finally asked Elisha, "What do you want me to do for you before I am taken away?"

"I want a double portion," Elisha replied.

Even while they were speaking, a chariot of fire split them apart, and a whirlwind transported Elijah to heaven. Elijah's mantle fell to the earth, and Elisha picked it up. He strode over to the Jordan River and slapped the water with that mantle. "Where is the God of Elijah?" he shouted, and the waters parted.

When Elisha came back across the Jordan River, the others ran up to him, saying, "Hey, you got the mantle! You got the anointing."

At least they recognized that Elisha got something. But from their next action you can tell their spiritual awareness left something to be desired. Though they knew God was going to take Elijah to heaven that day, they still bugged Elisha until he sent out a search party to look for Elijah's body!

Elisha knew better; he knew there was no point in looking, but "they urged him till he was ashamed" (2 Kin. 2:17). When they returned without Elijah's body after three days, Elisha said, "I told you so" (v. 18).

The actions of the sons of the prophets are typical of people who know God did something, but somehow they missed it. They go back later, trying to find it, but it's too late. They look for the "body" of what God did.

This story teaches us not just to sit there and watch from afar. Go over and get in on it while it is going on. A revelation from God will do you no good if you do not act on it. Elisha is the only prophet who did, and he's the only one we hear of again. The rest simply watched from a distance, not getting in on the greatest anointing of their day. Many Christians have been like that in the past and will be in the present-day move of God. Don't let God's work be aborted in your life.

Spiritual Abortion

If anything is worse than being uninvolved in what God is doing, it is starting out involved but allowing His anointing to be aborted in your life. It's a sure way to miss out on God's extraordinary power.

This spiritual abortion can happen in different ways. I know many people who were the most fired-up, would-be preachers you could ever see — ready to take on the world. But out on their own in the midst of the battles, they grew weary and quit, losing their anointing.

Sometimes pride aborts God's work in people, churches and nations. Some become arrogant with success, thinking they are the VIPs of the church. God's call had stirred within them. They had revelation and anointing. Then there was a problem; they cut the cord and lost their alignment with God's operation. Because they felt they didn't need their root associations and cut them off, pride entered. Today they are no longer in the ministry.

The devil will always try to abort God's plan for your life. When he attacks, strike back so intensely that the spirit of abortion will never attack you again. Wage war against that thing. Do not allow it to circumvent God's plan for you.

Importance of Spiritual Awareness

Although some people have sat under great men and women of God, they do not have spiritual wisdom to see that something extraordinary was going on. This has happened through history during the ministry of many great leaders raised up by God.

One woman who had gone to a Kathryn Kuhlman meeting said to me, "I went to one of her meetings, but I didn't get anything. I didn't get healed, and I didn't see anything. She didn't impress me at all."

How can someone sit in the middle of a great anointed meeting and not receive anything? Whose fault is it? Certainly it is not God's. He is there for anyone who wills to receive. It cannot be the fault of the spiritual leader through whom God is working when others all around these people are hearing from God. Most of the time, rebellion, hardness of heart or spiritual blindness prevents God's work in them.

By following the Holy Spirit the church of the end times can be aware of what God is doing. If Christians wax cold, it is because they have adjusted their consciences and minds to deceive themselves (Matt. 24:12). Some will call their coldness hot. Religious demons have a field day with these people. But you don't have to be among them.

Reformers of God

Another thing that will rob you of an extraordinary move of God is when God calls for change and you don't do it. In these last days the reformation move of the Lord is stirring again, as it has throughout history.

In Martin Luther's day, darkness and sin abounded in the land. The established church had waxed cold, substituting religion for relationship with God. They believed lies. Luther wrote out the truth in the Ninety-Five Theses and nailed them to the church door. He was persecuted for it. The religious leaders despised and fought his discussions. But many spiritually hungry people listened to Luther. They were tired of living in spiritual darkness and grabbed hold of Luther's truths from the Word of God. They were all labeled heretics.

As a reformation group of people, we must accept being misunderstood. We must be willing to undergo persecution from the world, from religious leaders and from some of our peers as we allow God to reform and give witness to His power.

Reformation means a time when truth is restored and re-established. It is a time when the course of future generations is changed. The apostle Paul was a reformer who was used mightily by God to change things in his day. His influence has lasted for two thousand years.

John Wesley was another great reformer. He brought England out of darkness. Wesley wrote in his journal that as he rode his horse one day to a town to preach, he became concerned that he was lost or offtrack with God because he had not yet been persecuted that day. He expected persecution for righteousness' sake and thought something must be wrong with him if he wasn't.

He jumped off his horse and knelt by the side of a rock and prayed. A farmer saw him out there in his field and threw a rock which hit Wesley square in the back. Jumping up, Wesley thanked God for the rock because then he was sure he was on track!

Wesley was one of the greatest reformers of church history because he had no fear of man. When he wasn't allowed to preach in any churches in England, he preached in the fields, and the masses came. One time he went into a town graveyard, stood up on a relative's tombstone and began to preach. Even though the religious folks despised him, the common man in England loved him. They were thirsty and hungry for the life of the gospel. God was never commonplace to him.

God's Might and Power

When true reformation hits, you will see the might of the Holy Spirit in action.

Many people think of the Holy Spirit as a cute, little, gentle white dove. That's how many painters picture him. That view is misleading. There are times when the Holy Spirit is gentle, and He can be easily grieved. But there are other times in the history of the church when He comes in with a roar. He is a mighty Person with all the power of God.

Acts 2:4 does not say that the Holy Spirit came on the day of Pentecost as a nice, little breeze that gave the disciples nice, little goosebumps. Thank God that it was more exciting than that. The power of God was manifested mightily in the Upper Room that day.

And when the day of Pentecost was fully come, they were all with one accord in one place. And suddenly there came a sound from heaven as of a rushing mighty wind, and it filled all the house where they were sitting. And there appeared unto them cloven tongues like as of fire, and it sat upon each of them (Acts 2:1-3).

That's the kind of Holy Spirit power that came over Samson the night he pulled the roof down on the Philistines. Samson killed more in his death than he did in his lifetime.

And it came to pass, when their hearts were merry, that they said, Call for Samson, that he may make us sport. And they called for Samson out of the prison house; and he made them sport: and they set him between the pillars.

And Samson said unto the lad that held him by the hand, Suffer me that I may feel the pillars whereupon the house standeth, and I may lean upon them. Now the house was full of men and women; and all the lords of the Philistines were there; and there were upon the roof about three thousand men and women, that beheld while Samson made sport.

And Samson called unto the Lord, and said, O Lord God, remember me, I pray thee, and strengthen me, I pray thee, only this once, O God, that I may be at once avenged of the Philistines for my two eyes.

And Samson said, Let me die with the Philistines. And he bowed himself with all his might; and the house fell upon the lords, and upon all the people that were therein. So the dead which he slew at his death were more than they which he slew in his life (Judg. 16:25-28,30).

The charismatic move of the sixties and seventies was the gentle side of the Holy Spirit, showing the love of God to a generation that sought love. Miracles happened, and it was a wonderful time with such a sweet presence of the Lord.

But today He is roaring in again like the Lion of Judah. His might and power will come through God's people again. It will bring a different style of preaching and administration.

Just because God is not doing things the same way He did ten years ago doesn't mean He's not the One doing them. Seeing Him as extraordinary, not commonplace, will keep our spiritual ears and eyes open to His movings. We need to be ready for the changes ahead of us.

God likes variety! He is the God who changes not, but He doesn't always work the same way. He is not boring. The diversity of His creation illustrates this fact. There are different races, climates and terrains. Not one human being is exactly identical to another.

We've talked about five different ways people can miss out on an extraordinary move of God: 1) treating God as commonplace, 2) standing and watching from a distance, 3) spiritual abortion, 4) not recognizing Him and 5) missing His call for change.

Our God is great. Our God is extraordinary. Let's be extraordinary with Him, doing things His way.

GOOD IDEA OR TRUTH

ONE INTERPRETATION of the Great Commission is this: "You are to preach the gospel to *your* generation" (see Mark 16:15-18).

During these end times our generation's responsibilities will be different from those of previous generations. We are going to preach differently, sound different and really be a "peculiar" people for God.

God's people are called peculiar throughout the Bible.

> Now therefore, if ye will obey my voice indeed, and keep my covenant, then ye shall

be a *peculiar* treasure unto me above all people: for all the earth is mine: and ye shall be unto me a kingdom of priests, and an holy nation (Ex. 19:5-6a, italics added).

For thou art an holy people unto the Lord thy God, and the Lord hath chosen thee to be a *peculiar* people unto himself, above all the nations that are upon the earth (Deut. 14:2, italics added).

For the Lord hath chosen Jacob unto himself, and Israel for his *peculiar* treasure (Ps. 135:4, italics added).

The same thing is said of the body of Christ:

Who gave himself for us, that he might redeem us from all iniquity, and purify unto himself a *peculiar* people, zealous of good works (Titus 2:14, italics added).

But ye are a chosen generation, a royal priesthood, an holy nation, a *peculiar* people; that ye should shew forth the praises of him who hath called you out of darkness into his marvellous light (1 Pet. 2:9, italics added).

The Hebrew word used in the Old Testament and translated in the King James Version as "peculiar" is *cegullah* [seg-ool-law]. Basically it means "wealth" (something so valued as to be closely shut up), "jewel, peculiar (treasure), proper, good, special."[1]

The Greek word translated as "peculiar" in the New Testament, *periousios*, is also defined as being "beyond usual, i.e., special (one's own)."[2]

In modern English, however, *peculiar* means odd, different and somehow flaky. Both the biblical definition and the modern definition will be right in the end times.

- *To God*, we will be separated from the world and be special, a treasure hidden in His heart.

- *To the secular world* — and, sadly enough, to many in the religious world — we will seem odd, different and weird.

It's perfectly all right to look odd or strange to the world if we look right to God. He likes peculiar people.

Peculiar people of God do things God's way — even if it looks weird or seems strange to others. In order to know which things are right for you, you must learn to tell the difference between a good idea and truth.

Just because an idea seems good does not mean it is truth. Oftentimes truth won't seem good to your mind or to your flesh. On the other hand, a good idea (without being truth) can be very appealing to the flesh.

For example, look at what happened to the Israelites when they decided they wanted a king. After almost four hundred years of being ruled by God's judges and prophets, they got a brilliant idea and demanded their own king.

They did this for one reason: to be like all the other nations around them (1 Sam. 8:19-20). They said to God, "Everyone else has a king. Why can't we have a king just like everyone else? We want a king." They sounded like a bunch of spoiled brats, didn't they? Little kids are just like that. Little Suzie comes running home from school saying, "Mommy, I have to have this new doll. Everyone else has one!"

Samuel tried to warn the Israelites about the consequences of choosing a man rather than God to rule over them, but they wouldn't listen to him. Samuel knew that under a natural king they'd have a stricter government, harder rules, more taxes and so on.

"A king will put you in bondage," Samuel told them.

But the people said, "Nay, but we want a king over us."

Then God told Samuel, "Don't worry about it. They haven't rejected you. They've rejected Me. Go ahead and give them a king — but I am not pleased with this" (see 1 Sam. 8:7-22).

Israel did not want to be *peculiar* in the modern sense of the word. It seemed like a good idea to have a king like everyone else. However, this was not truth — far from it. The truth was to continue to let God rule them directly, speaking through the representatives He chose. The truth was to have a theocracy, not a monarchy.

In these days we must not get so involved and spend time operating on good ideas that we miss the truth. I believe we have time only to do God's plan. Ministries must be careful not to allow themselves to become involved only in *good* ministry.

To be victorious, you must be in anointed ministry, in God's calling and plan. If you get into just good ministry, you will be distracted and slowed down. With only good ideas you'll never fulfill God's plan. With good ideas you tend to expand sideways but stay on the same level. You cannot move upward with God when you're so stretched out.

We must be a people who follow the truth, can penetrate darkness and penetrate the realm of the spirit and cause things to happen. That takes a special working of the Spirit of God in you and in the people you serve. You cannot penetrate the realm of the spirit as a corporate body without a divine focusing of the Spirit of God.

What if the apostle Paul had done things other than those anointed of God? He may have been doing good things that would not have gotten him into trouble, but he would not have been able to fulfill God's plan.

Dangerous Assumptions

Jesus said in the last days there would be many false Christs and false prophets (Matt. 24:11,24). Other parts of the New Testament also talk of false prophets, messiahs, teachers and brethren in the last days.

Did you ever wonder how so many false Christians or false ministries could be on the earth? The answer is that not everyone who ends up false started out false. Most of the false leaders began right and made a wrong assumption along the way somewhere. They *assumed* that something supernatural was from God and did not test the spirit that brought it. Then they fell into delusion. In the end they did not even follow good ideas, much less anointed ones.

In the charismatic movement, as in all of the past movements of God, some people have wound up in error through making assumptions. Others have taken God's truth and gone off the deep end with it. One example is intercession.

We've always had intercession in the church, but for a while it seemed to be fading out. Other ways to pray were fairly commonplace, but intercession wasn't. During the late seventies and on into the eighties, God began to restore our attention to the importance and power of intercession.

The Bible gives many instances of intercession. Abraham interceded for Sodom and Gomorrah; Moses interceded for the Israelites — not once, but many times; Daniel interceded for the Jewish people in Babylonian exile; Nehemiah interceded for the broken city of Jerusalem; Esther interceded on behalf of the entire Jewish race. Intercession has always been of God.

Intercession simply means intense prayer concerning certain people, places or situations. It means standing in the gap for others — rather than just praying for our own needs to be met.

But when God began to restore intercession, people in some places made assumptions and, therefore, made mistakes. Intercession became their total focus, and they did things that didn't line up with God's Word or Spirit.

Some would go home from intercessory seminars feeling superior to other Christians. Some even felt superior to their own pastors because now they were intercessors. They assumed they were on a higher spiritual plane because they may have received more understanding than someone else had.

People returned to their churches and tried to usurp their pastor's authority — because, after all, they really knew how to pray, right? Wrong! They assumed things that just weren't so. Instead of supporting their pastor in prayer, they got a burden to pray for the pastor. Then, of all things, they thought they should be the pastor! Some assumed offices to which they were not called. All kinds of havoc took place. How did all this mess occur?

They took truth — intercession — and assumed things with it. They thought that their new understanding of a long-time principle of God was equal to personal spiritual development. Knowledge and maturity are not connected that way at all.

You can have knowledge and understanding of the Scriptures, but you may not be mature. Unless you manifest the fruit of the Spirit and are faithful and obedient to do the works of Jesus, you will not be any more spiritually mature than someone without any knowledge. Knowledge doesn't mean spiritual maturity. It's what you do with that knowledge that determines just how mature you really are.

New revelation comes from knowing and understanding; spiritual maturity comes through changed attitudes, behavior and actions.

To some who learned about intercession, it was truth. It was for them, and God's calling was on them. Others took hold of it as a good idea then made assumptions based on their own desires, wills and experiences. They put themselves in an area of the spiritual realm where they did not belong.

The result has been many problems in local churches and for the church at large. Deception entered. Trouble came in. People began to teach and preach types and ways of intercession that were not strictly biblical.

In the end times, if Christians are not careful, they may assume callings and elections that are not from God. Then a spirit of deception and error will grab hold of their lives and pull them offtrack.

So we must be sensitive — not scared, not paranoid — but sensitive. We must be in tune with the Holy Spirit to discern the spiritual source of new ministries and restored truths.

If It Be of God, It Cannot Be Overthrown

The days following Pentecost were a wild time to be alive. Everything was changing right before the people's eyes. These apostle guys were running around doing all kinds of things that no one had ever seen before. Not everyone liked it either. In fact, most — especially the religious folks — did not like it at all.

When the apostles were brought in front of the Sanhedrin for trial, Gamaliel, a leader of the Pharisees and a doctor of the law, had some good advice for his peers.

> Ye men of Israel, take heed to yourselves what ye intend to do as touching these men...For if this counsel or this work be of men, it will come to nought: but if it be of God, ye cannot overthrow it; lest haply ye be found even to fight against God (Acts 5:35,38-39).

102

This is what we must be careful of in America — not to come against or abort an operation of God simply because we are not accustomed to the terminology, the methods or the style of the leaders.

The church needs to be careful not to accept everything that purports to be of God. Just because it's a good idea doesn't mean it's truth. Yet we shouldn't throw things out just because they seem different either.

One idea that may seem different is ranking. I believe there is a specific spiritual ranking in the kingdom of God to organize leadership service for the church as a whole, as we'll look at in the next chapter.

7

SPIRITUAL RANKING

ONE OF God's principles, I believe, is spiritual ranking. It's not to make one person in the kingdom of God better than another or so that one should lord it over another. Those with the greatest rank in God's kingdom will be the greatest servants of all.

In a natural army you have certain ranks and positions. People are put in those places to accomplish specific goals and to help others do the same. Each person within that army knows his position. If he is a captain, he doesn't take on the position of a general. If he is a general, he doesn't take on the position of a lieutenant. Everyone knows his place and stays in it. No one changes his post until a higher authority says to move.

So it should be in God's army. As part of His army, we must learn to respect the positions to which we are called and operate within that spiritual realm. Then the job will get done.

Let's look at the description of the warriors of Israel who had rallied around David.

> ...Expert in war, with all instruments of war, fifty thousand, which could keep rank: they were not of double heart. All these men of war, that could keep rank, came with a perfect heart to Hebron (1 Chron. 12:33,38).

These were men whose hearts were focused on one goal: to establish David as king of Israel instead of Saul (1 Chron. 12:23). Their hearts were "perfect"; they were not of a double heart in regard to their goal. Those with a perfect heart find it easy to keep rank, to stay "in battle formation" (NAS).

When God calls people to join His army today, some people will have difficulty taking their places in the ranks. People who think too highly of themselves will have problems as well as people who don't think highly enough of themselves.

It causes problems in God's kingdom when you try to take a post that doesn't belong to you. It also causes problems when you don't take the post that does belong to you. Once we find our place, we need to remain there until God promotes us or gives us new direction.

To stay in position, we must know how to deal with the pressures of battle in the spirit realm. We need to relate to one another in a way that will bring maturity into the church.

In one of my meetings the Spirit of the Lord spoke: "Many have already begun to walk down a deviant track." He went on to say that He was trying to woo them back into line and keep them in the proper order for the hour. He was trying to keep them from being led astray through their own wills and ways.

The Holy Spirit is calling Christians to humble themselves today and get back in rank so that He can salvage their callings and anointings. He is concerned that some will not come back to where they were called.

In a recent meeting the following prophecy came forth concerning setting His church in order for these times. In the following section I will present the prophecy as it was given. Then I will describe its implications.

A Prophecy Given by Roberts Liardon

There is turmoil in the governments of the world. But there also are spiritual governmental problems that are taking place. For many have created false governments, governments made of man's will and way, not of My plan nor of My anointed men.

Many have built systems by which they look so great. Many have built systems by which they stand secure. But they are false governments, and they, too, shall fall, as you have seen them fall in the natural in this hour. You will see false [spiritual] governments fall. You will see false elections [to spiritual offices] fall. Not all who have done this meant evil. Some did it through unawareness. I have spoken to them, but some have not heeded. Now I shall cause them to come down. For did I not say, I caused one king to come to power and one to come down? That [is the same] throughout My kingdom [as well as in natural kingdoms]. I am the promoter and the demoter, if the need arises. So do not. be concerned over the changing of governments because it is *My* Spirit performing that. For there are coming new governments, more anointed governments.

Yes, there are governments that stand accurate in My Spirit today, and I shall enhance them. They shall continue. So do not always be worried about whether this or that will go? But there are those who will not stand because I did not elect them. I did not build them. False governments shall come to an end.

You shall begin to see governing apostolic centers. They will come into power and deal with many things. These centers are governmental places that will regulate the atmosphere *above* the territory that they stand and call to. There is coming a greater governing anointing upon churches, [and there are coming] new churches in areas where men have not previously yielded. Where men have not wanted a church, I shall build a new one. But there are those who have waited for this time, and they have seen it from afar. Now it is among them. Now it is upon them. Now it is through their hands. They will begin to see these things manifest in their city and in their nation.

Yes, cities in America shall change. Yes, America shall have an eruption of good things. But they will come as the governing centers, which I have ordained for this time, come into power and into the operations I have needed for them to follow. So this is a new beginning of [spiritual] governments in the earth.

For, you see, I have planned that My apostolic gifts and My prophetic gifts and My ministry gifts will come into position. And I am building centers which they can work through and out of and come to a place and stand. And when they stand, they speak to a territory.

Thus, the end-times labor will be speeded up, and there will not be so much laboring in the flesh. But there will be those who will come by My leading to speak a word, to give a prophecy that I have given them. Thus, things will change, and they will change [seemingly] overnight.

And you will know that My Spirit is moving, and you will know that My will shall be performed.

Yes, there will be great opposition. What else do you expect? I am building these centers to cause My will to be performed, and the enemy does not like it. But we

shall win! And we will not see the defeat of
My purpose in this time.

Even for the North, the South, the East
and the West, you will see voices of great
men and women come on the scene that
you have not seen. For, yes, I have planned
at this time to release new ministry gifts.
I have planned to release fresh governments and fresh leaders. They shall come,
and they shall come, and they will not fade
away. So prepare your eyes and your heart
for the changes that you have heard about
this night.

You will see even national governments
come into concern over these centers that
I have established, says the Lord. Concern, because they will detect a higher
authority regulating things [an authority]
that they have never sensed or known before. And they will do things against the
churches, the centers, in the natural, but,
oh, they will not fall. They will stand and
laugh and go on through because they
know their God, and they want to do great
things — new authorities, new purposes,
new visions.

Apostolic Centers

Some people hear the words *governing* or *apostolic centers* and back off in fear without even
checking with the Holy Spirit as to the validity of
the concept. Nor do they check the Scriptures to
find precedents. Because they are unfamiliar
terms to the church today, they seem strange. And

because the devil has taken some things God was restoring in recent decades and turned them into bondage, some people are not open to the Spirit of truth in those areas.

History shows that in any of God's times and seasons of change, some Christians have fought the restorations of truth if they sounded unfamiliar. From the day of Pentecost, when the outpouring of the Holy Spirit set the religious leaders of Judah aghast, to Martin Luther, this same attitude has prevailed.

Human nature, which fears change, prevailed over the new nature within Christians. New things are only God's old things presented with a freshness for the time. God does not change (Mal. 3:6).

The work of "governing centers" is an extension of the many examples throughout Scripture where God used a person or group of people to speak His message for the time.

- Moses and Aaron to Pharaoh (Ex. 4-14)

- Isaiah and Jeremiah to people of Israel (see the books of Isaiah and Jeremiah)

- Daniel and his friends to the natural leaders of Babylon and Persia. These Hebrews prayed, studied and worked together in Babylon for more than seventy years (see the book of Daniel).

- The disciples who became known as the first apostles of the early church. Starting in about 70 A.D., their centers shook cities, towns and governments until Rome finally fell (in 476 A.D.).

- Martin Luther to the church of his day. Martin Luther did not come with a nice message that offended no one. He nailed his message to a church door and said, *"This* is the way we shall go."

Know Your Calling and Rank

In these days it is so important to stay in our own calling. It always has been important, but somehow, in this day and hour, it is even more strategic. In fact, it is dangerous for us to step into some other anointing and calling that God has not given us.

William Branham was a great healing evangelist and prophet of what has come to be called the Voice of Healing Movement of the 1940s and 1950s. But he stepped out of his calling and into error. He was a prophet, but he decided to teach instead. To this day there are still problems with churches in some areas because Branham moved out of his calling and tried to assume another office.

If God promotes you into a different calling, that is fine. But beware of looking so much at other people's callings that you try to step into those offices at your own will.

John the Baptist is a good example of someone who operated in his calling. He had a forerunner-ministry. He was born to prepare the way of the Lord. Shortly after he had done that, he left the scene. Even before Herod imprisoned him, John said, "He [Jesus] must increase, but I must decrease" (John 3:30).

That statement gives you insight into the man's character and into his understanding of spiritual

111

things. In the natural, men do not want to decrease; they want to increase. They want to stay out there doing what they are doing, only more so.

Here was a prophet of God whose entire ministry was to prepare the way of the Lord. And he knew it. At the Lord's arrival, his ministry would come to an end. He would have to fade from the scene so that people would come to the Lord.

His soul and his flesh could have given him a hard time over that. He could have felt rejected and gone into self-pity about not being needed any longer. But he did not. He knew what he was to do and what he was not to do. He stayed in his calling.

Not Knowing Your Calling and Rank

In the Old Testament we have an example of someone who did the exact opposite of John the Baptist. The actions of King Saul resulted in great death and destruction.

Not long after Saul had become king, the Philistines assembled to fight against Israel. They brought thirty thousand chariots, six thousand horsemen and foot soldiers like the sand of the sea.

The people of Israel were so terrified that they began to hide themselves in caves, cellars and pits. Even the soldiers in Saul's army were beginning to desert. He knew that if he did not act quickly, his entire army would be scattered.

Saul and the armies of Israel were camped at Gilgal waiting for Samuel to come and offer the sacrifice before they went to war. After waiting seven days for Samuel, Saul felt he could delay no longer.

And Saul said, Bring hither a burnt offering to me, and peace offerings. And he offered the burnt offering. And it came to pass, that as soon as he had made an end of offering the burnt offering, behold, Samuel came; and Saul went out to meet him, that he might salute him.

And Samuel said, What hast thou done?

And Saul said, Because I saw that the people were scattered from me, and that thou camest not within the days appointed, and that the Philistines gathered themselves together at Michmash; Therefore said I, The Philistines will come down now upon me to Gilgal, and I have not made supplication unto the Lord: I forced myself therefore, and offered a burnt offering.

And Samuel said to Saul, Thou hast done foolishly: thou hast not kept the commandment of the Lord thy God, which he commanded thee: for now would the Lord have established thy kingdom upon Israel for ever. But now thy kingdom shall not continue: the Lord hath sought him a man after his own heart, and the Lord hath commanded him to be captain over his people, because thou hast not kept that which the Lord commanded thee (1 Sam. 13:9-14).

Saul made an assumption. He second-guessed the Lord and thought it would be a good idea to get things moving without any more delay.

How did God react? Did He say, "What a good

idea, Saul! I wish I had thought of that"? No.

Saul was called and anointed to be king, but when he offered those sacrifices, he stepped outside his calling and assumed that he could also be a priest.

Samuel's reply shows us how God really felt about Saul's assumptions:

> And Samuel said to Saul, Thou hast done foolishly: thou hast not kept the commandment of the Lord thy God, which he commanded thee: for now would the Lord have established thy kingdom upon Israel for ever. But now thy kingdom shall not continue: the Lord hath sought him a man after his own heart, and the Lord hath commanded him to be captain over his people, because thou hast not kept that which the Lord commanded thee (1 Sam. 13:13-14).

Those who operate in great anointings and the power of the Lord must be careful not to become stiff-necked and hardheaded as Saul did. In these times ministers must maintain humility of spirit and the sensitivity to know exactly what the Lord is saying.

If you do make mistakes, the leadings inside your own heart can correct you if you are sensitive to the Holy Spirit. Or God may send a man or woman to help you become aware of how you are missing God. Remain humble so that you can receive what God is saying.

The word of the Lord came to Saul through Samuel, but he did not hear it. He did not perceive that he had made a mistake. His first reaction was self-defense, and his second was to blame "the people" (1 Sam. 15:13,21).

The door of correction was not open in Saul until the prophet kept bringing him back to what God had said, and he had to see it. Then it was too late (1 Sam. 15:24-26).

> And Samuel said unto Saul, I will not return with thee: for thou hast rejected the word of the Lord, and the Lord hath rejected thee from being king over Israel (1 Sam. 15:26).

Even then, Saul was more concerned over how he looked in the public eye than how he looked to God (1 Sam. 15:30-31). Saul begged Samuel to "honour" him before the people of Israel by going with him to worship.

David, Israel's second king, also sinned, but his heart attitude was different. He received the rebuke and correction Nathan the prophet brought to him. David repented and did not blame God for the death of the child born through the illicit union with Bathsheba (2 Sam. 12).

Zeal Should Operate Within Your Calling

Earlier we talked about the importance of discerning the difference between a good idea and truth. As you understand your spiritual ranking, you also need to be able to tell the difference between zeal and a calling. Young ministers, in particular, need to be careful. If you know your calling (1 Tim. 4:14), you'll not let zeal run you ragged —

taking you any and every place.

When I first began in the ministry, it went well. I was receiving invitations to go here, there and everywhere. But I kept getting checks in my spirit about doing certain things or going certain places. I had zeal to do it all, but I had to focus that zeal and not let it run me ragged. Wisdom and knowledge had to direct the zeal.

Those in the prophet's office, in particular, need to add one more dimension to staying within their callings — God's timing. For example, when you are driving along a highway and see a toll booth in the distance, you don't stop dead still right where you are and try to pay your fees. You slow down and *prepare* to stop at the proper place. When you see a red light in the distance, you don't come to a complete halt until you reach the intersection.

At times people in the prophetic office try to live in a situation which they have seen for the future. They take action prematurely and kill their ministries because they do not recognize God's timing.

I am seeing some young prophets do this today. They no doubt are called of God, but they are living in a realm where they do not yet belong. As time passed, they *would* be living there. But they do not want to take the time and make the effort it takes to get there, so their ministries are aborted.

I know one man right now who is not even serving God because he is mad at every other minister in the world. It's his own fault. He did not stay where God put him. You cannot go by what people prophesy over you. Perhaps that prophecy is true, but it may not be for right now.

The one prophesying over you could be saying things out of sequence, and if you take it for the now, it could cause problems in your life and ministry. There have been times when people prophesied over me, and I knew that what they were saying was right. But they gave the word as if it were intended for the present, when I knew in my spirit that it was for some other time.

Judge Prophecies

We need to judge prophecies so that we stay within our calling. We need to go to the Lord and make sure we know where those words fit. Do not allow great-sounding prophecies to cause you to assume a higher position in your calling before the right time.

I tried to explain this to the young man I mentioned earlier who was mad at preachers. I told him that he needed first to repent for blaming every preacher in the world for his mistakes. I told him that what had happened was *his* fault.

He said, "But so-and-so prophesied over me!"

Now the same person had prophesied over me, and I knew his ministry.

I told the young man, "That man has a calling, and he does speak the word of the Lord. I love and appreciate him. But his timing sometimes is inaccurate. I was in that same meeting where he spoke over you. What he said to me was right; but he was wrong in the time in which he felt it would happen.

"My head was all excited, saying yes, yes, yes. But inside my spirit, I had a no, no, no. So I went home, prayed about it and put it in a future time element. You did not do that. You just took what he said and ran with it."

The enemy will dangle a carrot in front of you to

entice you through doors prematurely; that is, if he cannot get you to deny your calling altogether. Every door of opportunity is not anointed. You have to watch that. Your zeal may make you want to run through doors without checking them out, especially if they look like wonderful opportunities.

Doors of Opportunity

Doors of opportunity must also coincide with God's perfect timing. This is so often where people miss it. What might have taken ten years to accomplish in the sixties may only take a year in the nineties. In the days ahead of us, timing will be crucial.

There may be some things that your soul has desired to do for a long time. But you may never be able to accomplish them because time will not be available to you. You must not mourn that. If you try to hold on to things in your personal life that are your desires but not God's desires for you, you will find the call of God aborted in your life.

Some things may look like good things to do. They might even look like great things to do. However, if they aren't in God's plan or timing for you, they will be hindrances to you and the calling He has placed on you.

Mobility Required, Not Security

We have to be a people who can move quickly as God leads. If God has called you to serve in His ranks in a full-time, public ministry, keep in mind that your ministry organization must be set up so that it doesn't dictate your actions completely. You must set it up so you are in control of your time.

The Holy Spirit may direct you to move on to another place. If you have built a ministry that controls your activities, you can't do this. That kind of control does give you a measure of security, a strong desire in every human being. But don't get so secure in the natural, soulish vein that you can't move when the Spirit says move. If you disobey God in that way, you will find the anointing lifting from your life and ministry. Because you're so concerned about security, He won't be able to use you as He wishes.

The organizational side of ministry is to be only an assistance to you, not a controlling factor. Don't allow the natural mechanics of ministry to dictate to you where you are to go and what you are to do.

If you allow the natural to control you, you will come up lacking in the day of judgment. On that day, when all things — good and bad — will be made known unto men, some will come up short. They'll inquire of the Lord, "Why? I was willing. I did things the best I could."

Then the Lord will tell them they concentrated more on the natural factors of their lives and ministries than the spiritual. He will say, "You allowed others to tell you what to do rather than Me."

That's something I don't ever want to hear. In the end it's all going to be sorted out — the good, the bad and the ugly. Anything we do that wasn't of Him is going to burn. I want to be like Jesus who stood before the Father and said, "I have brought you glory on earth by completing the work you gave me to do" (John 17:4, NIV). Jesus did exactly what the Father told Him to do *when* He was to do it. Everything He did was in divine order.

119

Many people already have things against their accounts in heaven because they have not kept their ministries in divine order and rank. Order is more than just keeping a holy camp. I hear people tell me all the time, "There's no sin in my camp." That's good, but that's not good enough. We also must keep that camp in the right place.

One time I was in Germany praying before a meeting. The Lord spoke to me about something that had nothing to do with the meeting. He told me to call a friend and tell her not to allow opportunity to control her. So I called her and wrote her a letter. When I got back to America, I took her out to lunch and talked to her again about this.

But it was almost too late. She'd seen all these opportunities before her, and she could no longer hear clearly what the Spirit was saying to her. She was so full of what was happening that she wouldn't listen to me. She would look at me, and it was as if she didn't even see me. "Hear me," I said to her. "Don't let opportunity control you."

"I hear you, Roberts," she said back. But she did not hear me. She was a million miles away thinking about something else.

God is trying to impart some messages to the body of Christ today that some people do not want to hear. They want to run their own races according to their own decisions and desires. False ministries may come in here.

What's Your Job Description?

I frequently use Kathryn Kuhlman as an example because I have studied her ministry and know more about her than about some other ministries.

People always want to know why she had such a great miracle ministry. What was it about her that was so different from everyone else? It was because she stayed in her calling. No one ever persuaded her to do something outside of what God had called her to do.

People wanted her to build buildings, to do this or that. They were trying to get her to do things that *they* wanted. She'd just laugh, look straight at them and say boldly, "I'm not going to do it." Some people got mad at her. One preacher friend of hers wanted to help her build a certain kind of building. He was convinced the idea was from God, but she was equally convinced that it wasn't. She would say, "It's not in my job description. God did not call me to do that. You may be called to do something else, but I'm called to do this."

Many people have had great callings like hers, but they were distracted. They went over into the good ideas and lost the truth. They never came into the full thrust of their ministry. It was aborted. It takes divine discipline to stay in the anointing. It does not come easily. You have to resist the pulls on you from others.

Always make time in your schedule to check in with heaven, whether you are in the ministry or not. Do not let yourself get caught up in the church-world's rat race.

God is trying to bring awareness to the church. It does not take much to get back in your calling — some prayer, some repentance, then learning from the mistake and getting back on the path God laid out for you. If you will do that, this can be your finest hour.

When God calls you into an office, a responsibility is placed on you, not only for the fulfillment of the office, but also to fulfill it in God's time and season, not yours. If those with ministry gifts today try to fulfill their offices out of sync with God's timing, they will not fulfill the responsibilities ordained for them in these last hours. This has become the problem with some people who accepted the callings of apostles and prophets.

Another way people will be led astray in these days is through assuming positions or anointings in which God never called on them to stand. This error leads to false ministry and false anointings.

Children in a natural home do not need to know everything that goes on in the house. They are loved to the uttermost, and all their needs are met. Yet there are things Mom and Dad know that children never need to know. That is not treating them badly. In fact, it is the very best thing for them.

There are things mature Christians are aware of that perhaps baby Christians do not need to know. Those matters are none of their concern, and they would not be able to deal with them anyway. If something is not within your calling, leave it alone.

If a five-year-old child tried to assume the responsibility of making a living for the family, can you imagine what would happen? The same thing is true in the realm of the spirit when people assume offices to which they are not exalted by the Lord. The result is danger to themselves and chaos and confusion to those caught in the situation.

Check Your Spirit

Many end-times false ministries will come from the assumptions of the soul. Arrogance will lead them into a position of greater popularity, instead of staying where they belong. The Holy Spirit told me to put a "check" in my spirit that I do not assume a rank, office or position to which He has not elected me. Men will try to place you in positions to which God never called you. So put a check in your own spirit, and take a personal warning from this. Know absolutely what your calling is.

Those called into the very difficult office of apostle in these times must be circumspect and walk a fine line in following God. Everything they do must be *from* God, *with* the Holy Spirit and *in* His timing, or they will create problems for themselves and the church.

Prophets also need to check and double-check their source and make sure it is *the* source, Jesus, the head of the church. Some people who were called of God have moved into a life of false ministry by prophesying according to gossip they have heard; others have by being suspicious or nosy.

That is different from missing it occasionally. False ministry is willful. A person sometimes continues reaching for "a word," even when the leading or conviction within his or her heart is against operating in a prophetic gift at that time. Perhaps the person felt pressured to perform; perhaps pride became involved in being looked up to as "a great person of God."

For whatever reason, people have continued to operate against a check in their spirits until they are totally off the right path. The words then bring death, not life. When these people lay on hands, instead of injecting healing and deliverance, they impart bondage of some kind.

Perhaps some of the people who have gotten off

on the wrong foot and who call themselves apostles and prophets really have the calling. But they have tried to administer it from their souls and not from the Holy Spirit's direction. Or perhaps they are trying to assume a level of anointing for which they are not yet ready and in which God is not ready to set them.

Just because some have missed it doesn't mean we throw out everything. If the principle is of God, we need to correct things and go on in His perfect will and plan. The ministry offices were set up by Him, not man.

Unity in the Ministry

There is a great harvest to be reaped in the nations. We need all the ministry offices to get the job done. If we remain ignorant of these rankings, the harvest will not be reaped fully. The enemy would love to abort the unity of the body of Christ by causing divisions among the offices. We must let the ministry gifts work together. Let the evangelist deal with lost souls. Let the pastor and teacher mature the body. Let the prophet declare the word of the Lord. Let the apostle father the works.

The enemy would love nothing more than to separate the ministry gifts and get them fighting each other. That would send the church into utter confusion. In these last days we are going to see the ministry gifts operating in unity as never before. But the devil is also going to fight it harder than ever. We must be aware of his devices and defeat his tactics.

Ministry gifts have different equippings. Don't get upset at the way God is equipping and operating through someone else if it's different from the way you do things. Let God be God. March only to the voice of your great commander.

Needed: Quality Church Members

A few years ago the Spirit of the Lord began to show me people in local churches who were trying to operate outside their spiritual realm. A "believer's anointing" would come on their lives strongly, but they all thought that meant they were called to be preachers, so they ran off to Bible school. Some were called to preach, but others were not.

Those who went to Bible school without a calling may have graduated and gone on to pastor or preach, but they flopped in the end. Now they are back in business feeling guilty, as if they failed God. They need not feel that way but should repent for assuming a calling that was not theirs. Then they should receive back the believer's anointing and run the race set before them. The believer's anointing is just as important as the anointing for an apostle or a pastor — only different.

In the end times we need quality church members. We need believers with believers' anointings. Those in the five-fold offices will not be able to do all of the ministry that is going to be required. The church needs members who know the Word — whether they have been to Bible school or not — and who know how to move in the ministry under a pastor's direction.

I will pray for people in my meetings until I fall over. I will do my best to help them. But people need to get it themselves. Sometime soon so many people will be coming to meetings (even in local churches) that the minister or pastor will not be able to minister to all the people by himself.

Right now I can't even handle everyone who needs ministry in my own meetings. On my most recent trip to the Soviet Union, there was no way I could lay hands on all the people. I had to pray *en masse* for thousands before me. Sometimes it's harder to pray that way than to pray individually because the needs are so great.

Helping people should be our goal. It will take dedicated, committed, anointed church members to help everyone. We need churches with trained ministry teams within the congregation. These teams will know the Holy Spirit. They'll know what to do and when to do it. They'll be people who can follow the authority of the pastor without getting out of rank.

Let's keep in rank and fulfill God's plan for these end times. God has divine ways of doing things, and if we'll do them His way, we will see mighty exploits accomplished for His glory.

8

DIVINE RELATIONSHIPS

SOMETHING ELSE we are going to see more of in these last days is what I call divine connections or divine relationships. By that I mean relationships between churches, between ministries and between individuals and even between nations.

In a natural relationship people get together because they like each other or because they have compatible interests such as fishing or golf. Divine relationships are connections that God puts together for His divine purposes and understanding.

Those who see these connections being made may not understand in the natural why these individuals or groups are associated. However, if God has ordained a spiritual union for His reasons, we had better go with the flow of it.

I am associated with people today whom I never dreamed would be my friends. Then there are others I believe I should still be friends with, but I'm not. Aborting these divine relationships is something we must watch for in the church in these last days. How will we know the people with whom God is trying to connect us?

> Wherefore henceforth know we no man after the flesh: yea, though we have known Christ after the flesh, yet now henceforth know we him no more (2 Cor. 5:16).

Paul was saying that from the time of Christ onward, believers would know one another by the Spirit. End-times relationships are to be based on the Spirit, not on whether we like the same sports or hobbies. Relationships are going to be established on divine common ground. Individuals, churches, ministries, cities, states and nations will be joined together divinely.

There has to be a deeper meaning to relationships between us than "Well, I'm a believer. You're a believer. We all believe this. Have a nice day." There has to be a commitment to one another that will stick through thick and thin. This will be hard on some people's souls, but the Holy Spirit is demanding a union and a commitment between His people. This union may be greater than any Christian generation we've seen, except possibly the first generation of Christians who even "had all things common" (Acts 4:32).

If you have some God-given relationships with people, and those relationships are not growing, then you need to get together and find out why. You need to make a commitment that from this time forward the relationships are going to prosper.

Examples From History

Let me give you an example of a divine relationship from history.

If you know of the developments in the Pentecostal and healing restoration movements of this past century, then you have probably heard of John Alexander Dowie (1847-1907) from Scotland. You may have also heard of a woman named Maria Buelah Woodworth-Etter (1844-1924).

Dowie had great revelation. He was an "apostle of healing," and he had a tremendous healing ministry in Australia and the United States. But there was no one who could minister to him concerning the accurate operation and administration of his gift and calling as well as his personal spiritual growth.

God chooses you to be the vessel of His power and glory, then He cleans you up personally as you grow in ministry. If you will not allow the pruning and cleansing of what is left of the old nature, then your ministry will be hindered and in some cases aborted.

Mrs. Woodworth-Etter was a Pentecostal pioneer. Like Deborah, she was a "mother in Israel" whom God used to accomplish great victories (Judg. 5:7). I believe God had arranged for these two to meet and develop a wholesome divine relationship.

Few people other than her could have spoken to Dowie honestly. It would have been difficult for most to see through all of Dowie's fame, all of his anointing and all of his strength and still tell him the truth. Few were able to understand the realm of the spirit in which he was operating and speak to him there.

But Mrs. Woodworth-Etter had given herself to the Lord and had gone through years of experience. She understood what Dowie was up against and what was set before him. She could have helped Dowie. Instead, the devil got into their relationship and aborted it. He brought them opportunities to get offended, and sadly enough Dowie fell into his trap.

Dowie had heard of how Mrs. Woodworth-Etter prayed for the sick and the sick were healed. He went to see her when they both held meetings in California at the same time. A friendship was started.

At Mrs. Woodworth-Etter's meetings, however, he saw people being "slain in the Spirit" or falling into trances. Apparently he didn't understand it. He went back to his meetings and spoke against her. Then she visited him personally, but they never spoke to one another again.

Is that not one of the saddest things you ever heard? Yet if we are not careful, there will be many opportunities in these times for the same thing to happen to us.

After a number of mistakes in administration and business, Dowie died in 1907 declaring himself to be Elijah, the restorer of all things. Why did he get so offtrack? I believe one reason was because the divine relationship that God intended for the benefit of both parties never came to its fullness. Dowie blew it by becoming offended.

Offenses prepare the ground for divine relationships to be aborted. Dowie and Mrs. Woodworth-Etter did meet on common ground, but it was the common ground of offense. They did not pursue the divine relationship, the common ground of the high calling.

Holding Together Divine Relationships

In Colossians 4:14 the apostle Paul wrote, "Luke, the beloved physician, and Demas, greet you." But in his letter to Timothy he wrote, "Demas hath forsaken me..." (2 Tim. 4:10).

Demas and Paul had had a divine relationship. Then that relationship, which God had arranged and placed together, was aborted. Demas was supposed to receive from Paul's anointing and to support the apostle. But Paul wrote that Demas was diverted, easily distracted from his calling, by things of the world.

Another term that can describe two parties in a divine relationship is kindred spirits. But what most of what the world calls kindred spirits looks to me like kindred flesh.

Now there's nothing wrong with having natural relationships, of course. But as we grow closer to the end, you are going to have to work at, cherish and spend time with those unions God has ordained.

End-times living demands spirit-to-spirit relationships, not spirit-to-soul. That is the only way the true fellowship of believers will be accomplished.

Coverings and Specialty Ministries

Some people keep telling others they need a "covering."

I believe that is true, but many times the covering that people end up with is nothing but soulish control or manipulation. I believe in a divine covering that comes through a divine relationship. There is a protection there.

Ministers often submit to people who are incapable of dealing with them on their level of spiritual maturity. I do not mean that you have to have some famous person as your covering. Some people are not well known at all yet are deep in the Lord and can be a blessing to you.

There are many churches that are deep in the Lord and not very well known to the church world in general. They will be good coverings. In the last days we need this kind of covering.

Demons have worked overtime to polarize people whom God meant to be together for a divine work in this time. The connections were not just for public ministry but for the purpose of assisting one another in some areas that are not in the public view. Many have gone through conflicts which would not have happened if they had the divine relationship with the other people whom God intended.

Divine relationships will be challenged and attacked but hold to what God shows you or has told you. It will be invaluable to you in these end times.

9

How a Spiritual Abortion Occurs

And then shall many be offended, and
shall betray one another, and shall hate
one another.

Matthew 24:10

JESUS IS saying that in the last days many people will be offended, betrayed and hated. It's not a very happy scenario. But "many" does not mean all!

You see, in these last days opportunities will increase for you to be offended. As you walk in the Spirit and take a strong, bold stand for Jesus, some people won't like you. In fact, they will hate you, harass you and persecute you. Persecution will come from fellow believers as well as from unbelievers. So we might as well get ready for it. But when the attacks start, you can overcome them if you don't hold on to offenses.

What does it mean to be offended? Probably every reader of this book has been offended at one time or another in your life. You've been emotionally hurt, used or abused in some way. Some kind of injustice has been done against you, whether you asked for it or not. Some people do ask for it, and they have no excuse. But still you must let go of the offenses.

Let me tell you how to let go of offenses. Just understand this one simple biblical principle: You do not have any right to be offended.

> Then came Peter to [Jesus], and said, Lord, how oft shall my brother sin against me, and I forgive him? till seven times? Jesus saith unto him, I say not unto thee, Until seven times: but, Until seventy times seven (Matt. 18:21-22).

> Ye have heard that it hath been said, Thou shalt love thy neighbour, and hate thine enemy. But I say unto you, Love your enemies, bless them that curse you, do good to them that hate you, and pray for them which despitefully use you, and persecute you; that ye may be the children of your Father which is in heaven: for he maketh his sun to rise on the evil and on the good, and sendeth rain on the just and on the unjust (Matt. 5:43-45).

In these verses Jesus lays out the plan quite clearly for what we should do when offended — forgive and love. We have no right to hold on to the offense. We are to forgive quickly and love one another. Then offenses will not lodge within us.

In these days to come, it's vitally important that we not allow any offense to trip us up. We will have more chances than we've ever had in our entire lives to be offended in these end days. Make the decision now *not to be offended*, no matter what happens.

That's right — it is a choice we must make. Walking in love and forgiveness isn't always the easiest thing to do. But according to God's Word it is the *only* thing to do. Let me give you an example of a wonderful opportunity I had for being offended.

Mistreatment and Justified Offense

Several years ago I preached a revival for a certain church. As the meetings started, the pastor told me and everyone else in the church that all the offerings would go to me. Well, I was happy to hear that because I really needed it. I was believing God at that point for one thousand dollars to come in to meet our monthly budget. We had been sowing seed, tithing and giving, and I was just asking God for that one thousand dollars to come in the offering.

The offering in that meeting totalled exactly one thousand dollars. I know that because the pastor told me so himself. Then when we got ready to leave, he told me he was keeping half of it.

That would have been fine if he had told me that

at the beginning of the meetings. If he had told the people in the services that half of their offerings would go to me and half to the church, then I would have prayed and believed for two thousand dollars to come in.

This pastor let it appear as if all the offerings were going into my ministry. He basically lied to me and to the people. To be perfectly honest, that offended me greatly.

I left those meetings with a rotten attitude, thinking, I'll never come back here again. I'll never enter this state again. Now don't get me wrong — I don't do meetings to get offerings. But in this case the people and I were lied to. I felt justified in being upset with this pastor.

I went home and complained and complained and complained about how I was treated. I told everybody I knew about it. But all my complaining and rehearsing of what happened to me only kept the offense alive. It was eating me up.

Finally, my grandmother got hold of me and set me straight. "What's wrong with you?" she asked.

"Haven't you heard?" I replied.

The gist of her response was, "Who *hasn't* heard?"

Then in her this-is-serious tone of voice she told me to sit down. When she talks like that, you know if you don't sit down, she's going to help you sit. So I sat down. I knew from the tone in her voice and the flash in her eyes that I was going to get it.

"Who gave you the right to act like this?" she asked.

"The pastor gave me the right by his actions," I told her.

Grandma started preaching at me then. "That's

a lie. You need to get out of this mess you're in. You are in sin; you're being distracted, and that's exactly what the enemy wants."

I wondered whose side she was on. "You're my grandmother. You're supposed to be on my side."

"I'm not on either side," she retorted. "You're both wrong."

Isn't it always wonderful to hear someone tell you how wrong you are in the midst of all your grumbling and complaining? We need more people who will be honest with us like that.

"I could have been offended for the rest of my life over the way I was treated when I moved to North Carolina with your grandfather to minister in some churches," Grandma told me.

"Have you ever been voted on and called a witch? Have you ever had the elders in a church vote against you? Vote that your husband could preach but you couldn't? You would have thought I had a contagious disease or something. They loved your grandfather, but they hated me.

"There would be times when God would tell me that I was supposed to preach! Well, thank the Lord, your grandfather would let me preach. Many of those people there and other ministers called me all sorts of names.

"They would see me coming and cross the street to the other side. Or they'd leave meetings and run home if I showed up. I prayed and knew things about them by the Spirit, and they didn't like it. They were afraid of me and hated me."

(She operated in the gifts of the Spirit, and they were not accustomed to such ministry in those early days of the Pentecostal movement.)

She continued, "I could have been offended at

everyone in that part of North Carolina. It would have looked as if I were right. But I refused to be offended. I just kept preaching and loving them. Roberts, you must do the same thing."

Believe me — I made sure I did what she said!

For those of us who live in the end times, there will be great opportunities to get offended. But if we are part of the glorious church, we must remain in the Spirit and not allow any offense to take hold of us.

Holding on to Offenses Has Consequences

What does holding on to offenses do? First, it distracts us from our destiny in God. If we allow an offense to live, it destroys our vision and the progression of our destiny.

In these times, if the devil can get us offended, he can abort the end-times works and the part we play in it. That is why Jesus warned us, "And then shall many be offended" (Matt. 24:10). He did not say this to scare us. He said it to make us aware of the dangers of being offended. He warned us so we can be stronger. We need to resist the attack of the enemy against the end-times church.

Second, holding on to offenses will cause us to live in a little circle of people that revolves around our offense and not around the Lord. The offense gets between us and our fellowman and between us and the Lord. It distracts us from going forward. We just maintain what we have.

Third, when we hold on to offenses, we lose our joy, our strength, our peace and our excitement in the Lord. We become tired, depressed, worn out. That opens us up to betrayal and hatred. *Now* is the time to forgive and forget, to let go of offenses — before they drag us into the stages of betrayal and hatred. The Bible says not to allow a root of bitterness to spring up in our hearts because it will cause trouble (Heb. 12:15).

> Let all bitterness, and wrath, and anger, and clamour, and evil speaking, be put away from you, with all malice. And be ye kind one to another, tenderhearted, forgiving one another, even as God for Christ's sake hath forgiven you (Eph. 4:31-32).

The fourth thing that happens when we hold on to offenses is that it breeds self-pity. As we continue to hold on to offenses, we will find ourselves on the hill of offense with others like us, all crying over how "so-and-so did me wrong." Once in that pit of self-pity, we will be drawn to a whole different group of people that we really don't need to be a part of.

It's called the Church of the Greatly Hurt. We begin to feel comfortable with that congregation. If we're not careful, we'll spend the rest of our lives in that hole of self-pity and destroy our earthly destiny in God.

Many people come to the leadership of their church for help. Then when the leadership tells them the truth and it hurts, they get offended. They leave the scene in a big huff, grumble and complain and get bitter. They think the only way they can be happy is if the leadership gets down in the ditch of sorrow with them and pats them on the back. A good leader refuses to do that because he knows it won't benefit anyone. A good leader tells it like it is — whether it hurts or not.

Fifth, holding on to offenses will lead us into betrayal and hatred.

> And then shall many be offended, and shall betray one another, and shall hate one another (Matt. 24:10).

When offenses lead to betrayal, they disconnect divine relationships and connections of God. In these last days there will be great opportunities to disassociate ourselves from one another. Instead, we must be stronger, wiser and bolder in the things of God so that we do not betray one another.

What is the opposite of betrayal and hate? It is love, of course. Instead of "many...shall hate one another," let us change that to "many shall love one another." Just because Jesus said many would go the way of hatred does not mean you are necessarily included. Some will be offended, others will betray, and then others will be betrayed. Some will even hate. But you do not have to be one of them.

Renew Your Mind

Jesus said, "See that ye be not troubled" (Matt. 24:6). Where does the trouble first hit you? In your mind, in your soul. Worry and concern affect your thinking and your emotions. Don't allow any offense to take root in your mind or emotions. If you do, your spirit man will also be affected. It will weigh you down and slow you down.

An *un*controlled, *un*renewed mind will mean defeat in this time. That should not put you in fear. But you need to know it so you will take steps to control your mind and emotions. Make them come in line with your spirit. Don't let them wander.

A controlled, renewed mind kept under the authority of the Word and the Holy Spirit will lead to victory in the coming times. We are not supposed to be led by our minds or our feelings.

Romans 12:2 tells us:

> And be not conformed to this world: but be ye transformed by the renewing of your mind, that ye may prove what is that good, and acceptable, and perfect, will of God.

How do you renew your mind to the Word of God? It's like a computer. What you put in will come out. The more of the Word of God you put into your computer bank (your mind), the more the Word will come out. The more you read, study and meditate in the Word, the more renewed your mind becomes. Then it becomes easy to think in line with the Word and the Spirit.

A Sign of Christian Maturity

A sign of real Christian maturity is how quickly you release offenses. Until the day we go to heaven, we will face opportunity after opportunity to be offended. But what you do with the offense is entirely up to you, as I learned so well from my grandmother! If it takes you six years to get over an offense, then you are just a baby. You are lacking in Christian maturity.

I talk to people who tell me about some horrible thing that someone did to them. It sounds as if it just happened yesterday.

141

"When did this incident occur?" I ask them.

"Oh, let's see, it was about twelve years ago," they say. "I don't rightly remember when."

That is ridiculous! Some Christians are professional offense-takers. They collect offenses and count them over and over again almost as memorials in their lives.

What would have happened if Jesus had held on to offenses during His years of ministry on earth? He certainly had every opportunity to get hurt and offended — even at the disciples.

He could have said, "Father, I'm mad at all these people. They are not treating Me right. After all, I'm *Your* Son! They keep calling Me the son of Beelzebub. Why don't You just zap them, Father, and get it over with?"

Jesus could have been offended at His own brothers, who thought He was going crazy when He moved into His ministry. He could have been offended at Peter, who denied he even knew Him on the night He was tried before Herod and Pilate (Luke 23:60-61).

In all these cases, Jesus refused to hold on to offenses. He chose to forgive and walk in love — even in His dying breath.

Then said Jesus, Father, forgive them; for they know not what they do (Luke 23:34).

Yes, Jesus was the Son of God, but He laid aside His heavenly rank and power when He came to earth (Phil. 2:7-8). He faced every temptation we do as human beings. He had to use His will to make choices to act like God or to act like a fallen man.

For we have not an high priest which cannot be touched with the feeling of our infirmities; but was in all points tempted like as we are, yet without sin (Heb. 4:15).

Love His Law

We will not be easily offended if we love the law of the Lord. His law is His Word, His principles.

If ye love me, keep my commandments. He that hath my commandments, and keepeth them, he it is that loveth me: and he that loveth me shall be loved of my Father, and I will love him, and will manifest myself to him (John 14:15,21).

Owe no man any thing, but to love one another: for he that loveth another *hath fulfilled the law* (Rom. 13:8, italics added).

In other words, the law is to love. Offenses are always going to be committed against us, particularly if we are a Christian in these times. But if we are walking in love, we forgive an offense the minute it happens. Then we forget and go on.

Tough Love

Jesus was full of love, yet He blasted demons. He cast out demons and hugged children. That is the way we are to be. Love has tremendous strength. The devil would like to get you thinking that if you are going to be a warrior, you cannot walk in love. The way he can do that is through a misunder-

143

standing in today's church about the love of God. Somehow we seem to think of God's love as "sloppy *agape*." People tend to confuse God's unconditional love with unconditional permissiveness. God is *not* permissive.

God says you can tell if someone is His child by the way He disciplines and chastises them (Heb. 12:6-7). Real love is tough. Real love does what is best for you, not what you think you want. Yet many Christians today think that if God uses you to correct them, then you are not operating in love.

One problem I face is people who have been hurt. They are professional hurt-people. The devil will see that they have opportunities to remain hurt and get hurt again if they keep hanging on to those offenses.

They say, "Well, I was hurt at this church. I was hurt at that church." Give them six weeks at the next church, and they will be hurt again.

Patting and pampering your hurt feelings will only reinforce the hurt, not get rid of it. Jesus came to heal the hurts and wounds, but you have to receive His healing and let go of the pain. Otherwise it cannot be healed.

Christians like to read Paul's epistles, but if he showed up in their churches, I am not sure they would listen to him. Pretty soon they would be talking about how he upset them and how mean and hard he talked.

The "nice" apostle Paul never existed. He was a tough, enduring prophet, who loved God and loved God's people enough to correct, instruct and chastise them when they needed it. Not everyone liked Paul. In fact, many people hated him. He had every chance in the book to be offended, hurt and bitter at all those who were constantly stirring things up against him, throwing him in jail, beating him, robbing him and leaving him for dead (2 Cor. 11:23-26).

Matthew 11:6 says:

> And blessed is he, whosoever shall not be offended in me.

Unbelievers, and sometimes even believers, may be offended at the way Jesus is in you or the way He operates through you. Sometimes that offense is a manifestation of jealousy. Be careful not to become jealous of how the Lord uses another person. We need to appreciate the way God works in other people.

In Matthew 13 Jesus tells about the parable of the sower. In it He talks of the ways in which the Word is sown, then He tells how it can be taken away by the devil or lost. One way the seed is destroyed is by becoming offended at trials and tribulations.

> But he that received the seed into stony places, the same is he that heareth the word, and anon with joy receiveth it; yet hath he not root in himself, but dureth for a while: for when tribulation or persecution ariseth because of the word, by and by he is offended (Matt. 13:20-21).

The Word of God falls on "stony places" in some people's hearts. When hard times come (as a result of the Word), these people become offended and give up.

145

Stony means "hard." Jesus is saying that His Word will not grow in hard hearts. A hard heart is easily offended at just about everything.

A hard heart builds walls against others. It is focused on itself, and when personal desires are not met, a hard heart becomes indignant. When trials and tribulation arise, a person with a hard heart screams out, "This isn't fair. I deserve better."

Welcome to life. Life here on this earth is not fair. It never has been and never will be. But we can live victoriously in the midst of it all if we decide to walk in love and forgiveness and refuse to hold on to those offenses. Refuse to allow your heart to grow hard.

What's the answer to all this? How do we keep ourselves from being offended? How do we get rid of any offenses we've been clinging to? Paul gave us the answer in 1 Corinthians 13:4-5 (NIV).

- Love is patient.

- Love is kind.

- Love does not envy.

- Love does not boast.

- Love is not proud.

- Love is not rude.

- Love is not self-seeking.

- Love is *not easily angered.*

Love is not easily angered. In other words, a heart that is soft with love toward Jesus and other people will not be easily offended.

The rest of the passage points out that love also does nothing to offend others! This requires us to live very carefully. Even so, some people will take offense at everything you say or do, and there's really nothing you can do to avoid it. However, we should try not to offend anyone, if at all possible. Make a decision to walk always in love.

Before he was born again, the apostle Paul did not care about anyone else's feelings. He did not even care about people's lives if they followed Christ! He held the coats of those who stoned Stephen (see Acts 7).

Yet after he was saved, he could tell the Corinthians:

> Who is weak, and I am not weak? who is offended, and I burn [grieve] not? (2 Cor. 11:29).

He was willing to change even his eating habits if they offended a brother.

> Wherefore, if meat make my brother to offend, I will eat no flesh while the world standeth, lest I make my brother to offend (1 Cor. 8:13).

I wonder how many of us would be willing to go that far? Jesus also taught about the seriousness of offending another Christian — even a little child.

> But whoso shall offend one of these little ones which believe in me, it were better

147

for him that a millstone were hanged
about his neck, and that he were drowned
in the depth of the sea (Matt. 18:6).

Summary

It is going to be important in the end times to
forgive easily and walk in love because the divine
relationships in which God places us can be torn
apart or forestalled by one person's taking offense.

Don't be one of the many who will be offended.
Make the decision to let go of offenses immediately
and walk in love and forgiveness. Then your heart,
your mind and your spirit will be free to serve your
Lord fully.

OBEDIENCE AT ALL COSTS

JESUS SAID that in the end times mankind would be as wicked as in the days of Noah (Matt. 24:38). In the Old Testament we read:

And God saw that the wickedness of man was great in the earth, and that every imagination of the thoughts of his heart was only evil continually. The earth also was corrupt before God, and the earth was filled with violence. And God looked upon the earth, and, behold, it was corrupt; for all flesh had corrupted his way upon the earth (Gen. 6:5,11-12).

The Lord said that man's imagination was continually evil and that the earth was filled with violence. Sounds like today, doesn't it? That gives us no excuse to sit back and wait for the rapture. We need to be doing what Noah did.

Noah was just and "perfect in his generations." He walked with God (Gen. 6:9). When God gave a command, Noah *obeyed* (Gen. 6:22).

A church of joyful obedience is desperately needed for these last days. God can use us fully if we give ourselves fully to Him. And that requires obedience. As we walk in obedience, His works will go into us and through us to accomplish His purposes in this earth. He desires to work a great work through us.

While Noah was waiting for the flood, he built an ark of safety. He stayed busy right up until the day that God told him and his family to get in that boat.

Today God is beginning to declare things pertaining to the end times for us. We are to be building things for God, for eternity's sake — no matter what anyone else thinks or says about us.

Notice that no one helped Noah except his own family. The neighbors and others who heard what this man was doing probably came to look and scoff. But no one helped him.

Imagine this scene: The neighbors were standing around laughing at Noah. "Hey, Noah, what's this thing you're building here? Sure looks weird."

"It's an ark," Noah replied. "God told me to build it because it's going to rain, and we're going to have a flood." Then he went right on about his business, trusting God's word. The taunts and laughs didn't deter him one bit.

"Right, Noah, and what's rain, Noah? We've never seen such a thing. A flood. You're nuts, man," they jeered back at him.

"God said He is going to bring water down from the sky and up from the ground and cover the whole earth," Noah explained again.

"Yeah, right, Noah! Whoever heard of water coming down from the sky? That's impossible. Don't you know that science has proven such a thing can't happen? Don't you know that, Noah? You're so stupid you don't even know that. You've gone completely off your rocker, Noah." They must have mocked and harassed him mercilessly.

Noah just kept on doing what God told him to do even as the people's taunts and jeers grew louder and louder. Noah didn't have it easy, but he remained totally obedient to what God had shown him.

When it comes to spiritual matters, the same thing will happen to the church. The world will mock and taunt us.

Keep Building the Ark

In days of great change, God does extraordinary things. Noah's day is our pattern for these times. People called Noah crazy, but he just kept on hammering. While they laughed, he kept on building. Almost every person in the Bible and in church history since Bible days who moved out ahead of the mainstream has been persecuted, laughed at and scorned — sometimes even killed.

So don't think it strange when people laugh and mock you for the gospel's sake. To be used in these end times, you have to keep obeying and keep building your ark of safety. Then when the storm comes, your ark will float. You will go over the top and not sink and drown!

We must build our lives in the Spirit the way God told us to build them for this day. We would do well to learn the lesson from Noah's life:

- He obeyed God instantly and without question, although what God said had never been heard of before in the history of the world. Talk about new and different! Water pouring down from the sky in a large enough quantity to cover the whole earth was a fantastic idea. Building a boat large enough to house this one man and his family, plus two of every animal species, sounded not only fantastic, but crazy!

- Noah operated by faith and not by sight (2 Cor. 5:7). If he had looked at past experience, current knowledge or current circumstances, the ark would never have been built.

- Noah maintained the divine relationships God had instituted within his natural family. He did not spend time regretting any natural friendships he may have had that had been lost, nor did he spend time in natural activities with old friends.

- Noah had to work vigorously to build the ark and to gather the supplies that God had told him to gather. He was single-mindedly focused on the task God had assigned to him.

- Noah built the ark *exactly* as God said.

- Noah *endured.* He persevered through everything to build his ark and get his family on it.

If Noah could walk with God during the ungodly times in which he lived, so can we in our time. No matter how evil or how dense the darkness becomes in the world, we are to be like Noah. We are to walk with God, to be *just in our generation* as Noah was in his (Gen. 6:9) and to be perfect (mature) and sincere toward God.

God saw that the end of all flesh had come before Him and that the earth was filled with violence through the people on it. But He made a way of escape for a just man and his family (Gen. 6:13).

Life in the Spirit

So what is our ark today? What is the safety of today? How can we fulfill our destinies with such an evil day about us? The ark of today is *life in the Spirit.* By walking in the Spirit, living by the unction of the Lord, we can be just and sincere toward our generation and walk with God — no matter what is going on around us.

Life in the Spirit is not a suggestion for you. It is the place where God calls us to live just as Noah and his family were called to live in the ark. When the rains came and the waters hit the ark, it floated above the flood all the way. When the evil waves of the day come toward you, you will be able

153

to float above all of the garbage — if you have built your ark in the realm of the spirit.

Also, remember that Noah built his ark as God described it to him. What if Noah had changed the specifications a little? What if he had built a luxury liner instead of the ark of the Lord? Perhaps he wanted a swimming pool on it, or maybe he wanted to take some friends with him. What would have happened?

The luxury liner would have sunk. A boat filled with his ungodly friends would have sprung a leak. It is only the ark of God that will go through.

Some people like to build quick boats. They want to throw something together and "trust God" for it to work. But God does not work that way. That attitude is what has caused a lot of preachers, churches and ministries of the past to be covered up with the flood waters of their times.

They built a rubber raft or a prestigious luxury yacht instead of a strong, stable ark that could survive the storm. Your ark must be able to survive the clouds, the rain, the forces of the darkness and the pounding by the enemy.

Hunger for God

The first step to building your life in the Spirit is to make sure you have a hunger for God. If there is no hunger for God, there will be no seeking of the Spirit.

If I were on the second floor of a two-story house and I wanted to get something to eat, I would not sit down on a bed and wait for the food to float up to me from the kitchen. I could sit on the edge of that bed all day long and wait, confessing, "I'm waiting for the food to come. I believe it's coming. I am waiting for the manifestation." That would not cause the food to come up to me.

That is not the way natural hunger is fed, and neither will food in the Spirit come that way. There has to be a desire, a hunger in your spirit man. Then there has to be a seeking. Natural hunger would cause me to walk down the stairs and into the kitchen. If you hunger after the things of God, you will get up and go after them.

Christians do not realize, however, that spiritual food is actually more necessary than natural food. Without natural food the body will suffer malnutrition, develop diseases and eventually die. Without spiritual food the *real* you, the spirit being within the body, will also suffer from spiritual malnutrition, be susceptible to spiritual attacks and diseases and eventually die.

If you keep attending anointed meetings and putting the Word into your system, you will get an appetite for spiritual food. In fact, you will become addicted to heavenly things. That is the only addiction that will not kill you. Instead, it will allow you to live above the wickedness of the day.

Life in the Spirit is not just a wind that blows through the room. It is not just staying in anointed meetings, although that is a good place to start. Life in the Spirit must operate at home, on the job — wherever you may be. You must be in the ark at all times.

When you are by yourself or with your family in everyday situations, you can tell whether you really are spiritually hungry or not. It is easy to be hungry in anointed meetings or when surrounded by strong, spiritual people, but in your private life, are you still hungry for God?

If you want to see whether you have a spiritual hunger, ask yourself why you read the Bible. Do you read it just to teach or preach a message? Do you read it for your personal life? Or do you read it because you want to know about God and His ways *more* than you want to watch television, read other books or spend time in other activities?

Thirst for God

David walked in the Spirit. In Psalm 63 we read his words:

> O God, thou art my God; early will I seek thee: my soul thirsteth for thee, my flesh longeth for thee in a dry and thirsty land, where no water is; to see thy power and thy glory; so as I have seen thee in the sanctuary. My soul followeth hard after thee: thy right hand upholdeth me (Ps. 63:1-2,8).

David was not just sitting on his kingly throne waiting for God to come through the room. He got up and sought after God. To build your life in the Spirit you must seek God, follow hard after Him, thirst and long for Him.

You may say, But I don't feel like that right now. I love God, but I'm not into all of that. He saved me. I'll be a nice church member. I'll pay my tithes. I'll sing in the choir. But that's it. I'm not ready to do anything else.

That is not building an ark. That is compromise. Some people think that wishy-washy kind of Christian life is walking in the Spirit. That is why they do not know the Holy Spirit when He shows up.

In these days we have to lean more and more on the things Christ did for us in the Spirit. We must rely more on spiritual things than natural. When people rely on things of the flesh, they fall apart. They begin to die.

The day you quit going after God is the day you start losing your life in the Spirit. The most important step is developing your spiritual hunger and thirst. Jesus talked about this principle in the Sermon on the Mount.

> Blessed are they which do hunger and thirst after righteousness: for they shall be filled (Matt. 5:6).

If you hunger and thirst for righteousness, Jesus said that God will fill you. Righteousness is a necessary part of life in the Spirit. Jesus also said that God is just as eager to fill our hunger for the Spirit.

> If a son shall ask bread of any of you that is a father, will he give him a stone? or if he ask a fish, will he for a fish give him a serpent? or if he ask an egg, will he offer him a scorpion? If ye then, being evil, know how to give good gifts unto your children: how much more shall your heavenly Father give the Holy Spirit to them that ask him? (Luke 11:11-13).

The Spirit Is Life

Life in the Spirit is not a show, not something

157

you put on and take off. In Romans and in Galatians, Paul talked about life in the Spirit. He did not say boredom or bondage in the Spirit; he said *life*. There will be things you cannot do anymore, but it will not be because God is taking things away from you. He is just getting you into divine order so you can live in the Spirit.

The only time some people get into the Spirit is when they are in trouble. When there is a dramatic problem in their lives, they may take two days off work and shut themselves in their prayer closets where they have not been for months or years. Then they will pray in the Spirit in strange utterances because they need an answer. It won't accomplish much of anything.

God has planned for us to stay in the ark *all the time*. If you have ever spent time in that realm, can you remember how you got there? Do you know what it felt like when you came into that realm? Do you remember what it felt like when you got the victory, the assurance that God had answered your prayer? Remember how happy you were?

When people looked at you and said, "Well, we hope everything works out," you were able to say with all confidence, "It's all right. It will be fine." You had prayed it through, and you knew that you knew that *you knew* everything was going to be all right. That is the ark of today.

Life in the Spirit is not a bubble away from the world. Life in the Spirit gives us the power, the protection and the authority to go to the corrupt world as Noah did and preach what God is saying today.

Noah kept saying, "The end is coming. A flood is coming, and it will destroy everything that is not

OBEDIENCE AT ALL COSTS

in the boat. You had better get in this boat because this is the boat of safety." He preached that for years while he kept building (2 Pet. 2:5).

The world desperately needs our message. I believe that if you do not live in the Spirit, you will not live happily in these days. I do not say this to bring fear but to show the urgency of our times. Without the ark of the Spirit, tragedy will be your friend.

God Will Not Always Strive With Man

And the Lord said, My spirit shall not always strive with man (Gen. 6:3).

That verse, of course, applied to God's dealing with mankind in Noah's day. However, the same principle applies in this day.

There comes a time when God stops dealing with the hearts of individuals, with the congregations of churches and with nations. That time comes when they have heard the truth and heard it and heard it. Yet they have refused to change, to act on the truth they have received.

Ministers today must learn to go on when God says it's time to get in the ark. If your congregations do not go on with you, you must go on anyway. Are you going to remain off the ark and drown simply because the rest will not go with you? Just because someone gives a large amount to your church and wants to tell you how and what to preach, are you going to miss the ark?

You had better obey God. You had better be like Noah. The apostle Peter called Noah "the preacher of righteousness" (2 Pet. 2:5). What does that mean? That means he preached the right way to go. He preached the right way to walk.

When he hammered in nails, and they said, "You're crazy," he answered, "I'm normal. The day is coming when you will realize that you have not been too smart."

When you say, "I know I'm right," and you are preaching things that sound different, many people around you have a tendency to accuse you of pride. People get nervous when you have a bold confidence.

I picture the situation like this: All of us are in ditches full of muck and mire, but some people find the way out. They are standing on the bank, cleaned off and telling the rest how to get out of the mud. But the rest think of themselves as normal. Living in the muck and mire of the world is what they are used to, and to them the clean people look weird. If the people on the bank are not careful, the others will convince them to get back in the muck and mire.

The same thing happened when you got born again. All of your friends in the muck and mire of sin thought you were weird for getting cleaned up and out of the ditch. Some new converts actually are convinced to get back down in the ditch.

In the Christian life there is another ditch. Perhaps it is not filled with carnal sins. But it *is* filled with the muck and mire of religious traditions and doctrines of man. It is filled with self-righteousness. It is filled with gossiping, criticizing the pastors, grumbling and complaining about fellow Christians. It is filled with the pride of thinking that the way you are is normal and that you must pull down with you those who live differently.

In these times we do not just have minor headache demons coming against the church. These are terrorist spirits. They are strong, and they know what is going on.

But demons should not be able to see and know better than the church what God is doing. If we live in the realm of the spirit, we will know more than they. The Holy Spirit will reveal to us not only what God is doing but why He is doing it. We should not get into the seeing-demons-everywhere syndrome. On the other hand, we had better not be ignorant of the enemy's devices either.

We are already seeing the rains begin, like the destructive rains in the days of Noah. We are seeing confusion and distraction coming in waves across the world and across the church. Some ministers are not building arks. They are building pulpits and empires instead of arks, and they are dying. That is why some ministries are falling apart.

Time is short. We do not have time to play games or to build the wrong kind of boat and start over. We do not have time to be unholy, unclean or unrighteous, following the demands of our soul or flesh.

Some ministers have preached that a new move of God was coming, but when it came, they did not recognize it. They are not getting in on it. They did not get in the boat. Now they are fighting those who did!

When you build an ark, you have to take one step at a time. You pound that nail in and make sure that board is secure. Then you put the next nail in place and pound it in securely. You do that so that when the time comes to get in the ark, God will shut the door, and your ark will sail.

If you do not build it right — if your workmanship is shoddy or half-secure — God cannot shut your door. Your ark will be part flesh, and it will spring a leak when the going gets rough.

Let's stay in complete obedience to what God has called us to do. Let's build that ark of safety — life in the Spirit — and then we'll sail on into these last days with a smile on our faces, excited to be doing the works of God.

It's fun to be alive today. We have the opportunity before us to change the world. We will do it in the Spirit, though, not the flesh. Life in the Spirit will help us live victoriously and adventurously for Jesus in these concluding moments of this dispensation.

11

CHANGING YOUR CITY

IN NOAH'S day everything on earth was destroyed. Only Noah and his immediate family survived. Millions of people died because they refused to believe what Noah said about the flood coming. He tried to warn the people. He continually begged them to repent, but they did not. And they all perished.

But God promised Noah that He would never destroy all of humanity like that again. I don't believe God's first choice is ever to destroy a city or a nation. Yes, He's a God of judgment, but He's also the God of mercy and justice. I think God would rather see a city change than be destroyed. He's not willing that any should perish (2 Pet. 3:9).

Reformers who know God's might and power will do what it takes in prayer, praise and preaching the Word to change the spiritual climate of communities, cities, states or nations.

Did you know that cities have a voice? In Genesis 18:20-21 we see this.

And the Lord said, Because the *cry* of Sodom and Gomorrah is great, and because their sin is very grievous; I will go down now, and see whether they have done altogether according to the *cry* of it, which is come unto me; and if not, I will know (italics added).

Every city, every nation has a voice. But not all of them have a righteous cry coming forth from them. Some are like Sodom and Gomorrah — all that was heard from them was sin and wickedness.

God hears those cries — whether they are wicked or righteous — and He responds accordingly. We have an example of this in Exodus 2:23-25.

And it came to pass in process of time, that the king of Egypt died: and the children of Israel sighed by reason of the bondage, and they cried, and their cry came up unto God by reason of the bondage. And God heard their groaning, and God remembered his covenant with Abraham, with Isaac, and with Jacob. And God looked upon the children of Israel, and God had respect unto them.

God heard the cries of His people for relief from Pharaoh's cruelty. He called out Moses to be their leader and led them out of Egypt in victory.

As I travel around the world, I notice that certain cities have their own voices. Each seems to have its own distinct flavor or reputation about it. Oxford, England, is known as the city of intellectuals. Tulsa, Oklahoma, is often referred to as the buckle of the Bible belt. Paris is known for its art and fashion. Venice, for romance. San Francisco, for its homosexual community. The reputation of each city is the world's way of sensing which principalities rule over those places.

Either a wicked spirit rules and affects the voice of a place or the voice of the righteous saints does. It's up to us which one reigns. As believers gain understanding and revelation from the Lord, the cry from our cities can be changed from wickedness, bondage and oppression to righteousness.

As the time of the end approaches, cities and nations will be found either wicked or righteous. I don't know about you, but I intend to do everything I can to make sure that my city's voice is one of righteousness.

A Divine Stirring

When you begin to change the voice of a city, it often starts out small. However, the change will grow as you stay in the battle and allow God to work through you.

In telling the story of the early church, Luke wrote:

Now while Paul waited for them at Ath-

165

ens, his spirit was stirred in him, when he saw the city wholly given to idolatry (Acts 17:16).

Paul was stirred over the sins of Athens. Are you stirred over the sins in your area? There must come a provoking in your spirit, a righteous indignation against the wickedness of sin in a city. This stirring will cause action.

Instead of saying, "Well, there's some kind of wickedness here, that's for sure. Father, bless this city and change it," we need to find out which spiritual forces are over that whole city, attack them and bring about change.

We attack spiritual principalities over cities for various purposes:

- To change the spiritual climates of the cities.

- To pull down spiritual darkness, allowing people there to see the *real* Jesus.

- To bring revelations from God in order for Him to do His works in the people, to train them and to launch some of them out into other cities.

In the book of Acts we are told of Philip's going down to Samaria to "preach Christ unto them" (Acts 8:5). He did not go down there to complain about the problems in Samaria or to criticize and condemn the Samaritans. He went there to *preach Christ* to them. And we see what happened immediately.

And the people *with one accord* gave heed unto those things which Philip spake, hearing and seeing the miracles which he did. For unclean spirits, crying with loud voice, came out of many that were possessed with them: and many taken with palsies, and that were lame, were healed. And there was great joy in that city (Acts 8:6-8, italics added).

A city is made up of people, not buildings. Our goal, like Philip's, is to help people live the abundant, victorious life that Christ has for them. No matter what has happened to them, Jesus wants to help people live in victory. That needs to be preached to the cities of the world.

The reason so many cities and nations are desperate and in trouble is because no hope is preached to them. They see no way out of their problems. They have no solution for the crime and drug problems that are running rampant.

A Twofold Process

In many cities, especially in America, people are desiring to change their areas. Most of the time they mean well. But they miss the strategic ingredient: changing the spiritual climate. Instead, people only concentrate on trying to change the natural element. They go out and march, holding demonstrations and so on.

It can do some good temporarily. The symptoms of wickedness may clear up, but sooner or later they will burst out somewhere else. You must find the cause of the problem and eradicate it. The cause is Satan's strongman over the place.

> How can one enter into a strong man's house, and spoil his goods, except he first bind the strong man? and then he will spoil his house (Matt. 12:29).

If a satanic strongman has a grip on a town or city, you cannot change that city's voice without binding the demon over the city. That is why it is important to know which strongman is over a place. Then you can do spiritual warfare to change the area.

To change a city, you must do two things in order: work in the spiritual realm and then work in the natural. One without the other will not cause a permanent change to come to the city. Christians tend to do one or the other but not both. They either do things in the natural and do not cry out to God for the place, or they do spiritual warfare and never do anything in the natural.

A pastor friend of mine has a church in a city where violence had been exploding. The suicide rate was also skyrocketing. They did not know what to do about it. One Christian policeman suggested to the city leadership that a prayer warrior needed to ride with the police to help deal with the problems.

To my friend's shock, as well as to the shock of many in that city, different ministers were allowed to ride with the police on patrol. I advised him to keep his people praying and not lose that door of opportunity that had been opened to them. We shall see that city changed.

That is a great example of getting involved in

both the natural and the spiritual. I believe there are going to be more such doors opening throughout the world. The cities of the world do not know how to handle the problems they are facing. Only God's people can truly help them.

When the door to a city opens, we need to be ready to keep it open. Pray to get the door open, keep it open in prayer, and keep praying through to the victory. Things will change.

Philip went down to Samaria and preached Christ to them. While he was there, he healed the sick and cast out devils, and the city rejoiced (Acts 8:6-8). When we provide answers to the problems of the cities of the world, there will come a rejoicing and an acceptance of Jesus. The city's voice will change.

Divine Plans and Direction

In Luke 19 we find a story about how Jesus dealt with the city of Jerusalem.

> And when he was come near, he beheld the city, and wept over it, saying, If thou hadst known, even thou, at least in this thy day, the things which belong unto thy peace! but now they are hid from thine eyes. For the days shall come upon thee, that thine enemies shall cast a trench about thee, and compass thee round, and keep thee in on every side, and shall lay thee even with the ground, and thy children within thee; and they shall not leave in thee one stone upon another; because thou knewest not the time of thy visitation (Luke 19:41-44).

God had a plan for Jerusalem, but the city did not recognize it. The consequences were severe, and Jesus wept for the city.

God has definite divine plans for certain cities. Christians in those cities need to tap into that plan. You do this by speaking out the word of the Lord, by preaching the Lord's plan for them. Many cities do not have direction. There needs to be a spiritual leader who gives direction to the city.

Determine that the Lord will not have to say this to your city: Because you did not know the time of your visitation, you missed what God intended for you. Pray that your city will not be like Sodom and Gomorrah or Athens or Jerusalem.

Today is God's day of visitation to the cities of the world. Now is the time when God is going to visit the believers in cities. He wants to use them to help manifest His purposes in the earth. Remember that we do it in two ways: laboring in the spiritual realm and walking out the changes in the natural.

We have to go out where the sinners are because born-again people can't keep getting born again and again and again. Get out into the sinners' world and preach Christ to *them*. Invade the world of sinners, and they will become a part of God's big world.

Jesus said to Jerusalem, "You don't know what could have happened here. You have no idea what God had planned for you. You have missed the things that belonged to you."

We must grab hold of the vision that God has for our cities. As we understand His divine purposes, then we can make changes.

Occupy With Power

We are not just to occupy our cities casually until the Lord comes. To occupy does not mean we simply "let our little lights shine."

We have the idea that we're to light our little candles and sit by their little flames waiting for people to come by. End-times lights are not little candlelights. They are mega-spotlights. We are going to illuminate the world with the power of God. The church is going to light up the darkness. That will take powerful spotlights, not little flickering flames.

Some will say, "Turn the light down. It's too bright. We don't want this bright light. What happened to that nice, little light you Christians used to have?"

Others will try to run from the light. Let it shine out there anyway. We are the light of the world, the salt of the earth, and we are going to change the voices of the cities of the world.

As our lights shine brightly, governments of the world will get nervous about the end-times army of God. There will be endless discussions about what Christians will do next.

God likes to hear His people pray, prophesy and declare that nations shall be saved. That is the cry God will come down to check out. And when He comes down, the city or nation will shake even more because of His glory and His power.

The Law of Faith

Another thing that works in taking cities is *faith*. The law of faith helps you get healed and brings prosperity to your life. Faith has been taught a lot in the past two decades; however, many people have developed tunnel faith — faith just for certain things. Or they have selfish faith. All they think about is what faith will get for them. We need to grow up and realize faith is not just to get things.

We need a revelation that the law of faith works on behalf of cities. We are not to be as one that fruitlessly "beats the air," but as one determined to win the prize (1 Cor. 9:24,26). We must believe that what we say has an effect over our cities. What we declare about our cities helps change the climate and voice of the cities.

When you first pray to change the voice of a city or a nation, your confession may not match up to what you see in the natural. What you are calling into existence is what you see in the spirit.

Abraham is a model of faith for us. Abraham kept believing what God said — that his descendants would be as many as the stars. That takes a lot of faith when you don't have any children. We must believe for our cities as Abraham believed his promise from God — even before its fulfillment. Through faith and patience we inherit the promises.

Romans 4:18 describes Abraham's faith:

Who against hope believed in hope, that he might become the father of many nations, according to that which was spoken, So shall thy seed be.

When you believe a promise of God that has not yet come into manifestation, you are not believing

172

a mental picture. You are not believing a group of Christians' opinions. You are believing for God's divine purpose and call to manifest. You are believing that the vision God has given you will come into existence.

That is what we need to be doing for our cities and countries. We see from the Bible that we can change the voice of our cities, and we know that is God's will for our time. Therefore, we believe that the picture of wickedness we see with our physical eyes will turn to righteousness.

Now faith is the substance of things hoped for, the evidence of things not seen (Heb. 11:1).

We must do what Abraham did: "And being not weak in faith, he considered not his own body now dead" (Rom. 4:19). We *consider not* the way the city looks now or the fact that it seems spiritually dead. We consider the promise and the vision, and we call that into existence.

We believe that what we have seen, what we are sent to do — change the course, the voice, of the city — will come about in the now. We believe like Abraham, who

being fully persuaded that, what [God] had promised, [God] was able also to perform (Rom. 4:21).

When we go into territorial spiritual warfare, we must be fully persuaded that what we know by the Spirit shall come to pass. We must also watch what we declare, that it really is the word of the Lord. If your prayer isn't the word of the Lord, God might only give you what you ask for, instead of releasing everything He desires for the city.

Someone told me, "You can't take whole cities. You can only take little parts of them." Small faith makes statements like that. Strong faith, end-times faith, takes the whole thing. Our faith can take the cities and nations of the world!

The Role of Gifts of the Spirit

The gifts of the Holy Spirit also play a part in taking cities for God. Many times we think the gifts of the Spirit are only for individuals. But the Lord can help you change the voice of your area through His gifts. For example, the gift of faith will come at times and give you the spiritual breakthrough you need in prayer for a city.

I was at a church once that had gone through some trouble, and a tremendous church split resulted. The pastor is a great pastor, and he had asked me to speak there around the time all of this began to happen. I preached one night, and he asked me to stay for another night.

I knew God was in it, so I stayed. While I was in my hotel room preparing for the second service, the Lord said, "Preach to them tonight that they will have ten thousand hungry believers in their church."

That was a seed that needed to be deposited in their hearts because their vision had begun to die. Their hope and their faith were losing ground. The thing that had happened shocked everyone. This event even caught the minister off guard, and he was so sad.

174

At lunch the next day he talked about quitting. I tried to do what I could to exhort and build him back up, but that first night I had not gotten the breakthrough in the service that I knew the Lord wanted.

On the second night, however, I began to preach God's vision for the church. Preaching was very hard because the atmosphere was so heavy. Every time I told them to believe God for ten thousand hungry believers, the spiritual atmosphere got heavier and heavier.

They have a building that seats that many people. It is a private convention center really. It was built because God ordained it, not because man thought it up. When God ordains a building that large, it means every seat should be filled.

The devil attacked them and tried to stop the operation before it really got started. I kept pressing the anointing and pressing myself. I said what God had told me in every way possible. I yelled it; I whispered it; I said it slow; I said it fast; I said it with every bit of energy I had. But I still wasn't getting a breakthrough.

All of a sudden the gift of faith came into me, and the gift spoke forth that statement. Those words came out of my mouth and were spoken out into the atmosphere over that building: "There *will* be ten thousand hungry people in this church." And that time, it was as if two or three walls fell away in front of me.

People began to rejoice, and hope came back into them. The seed God planted took root, and they began to build back up again. The gift of faith helped save that church. In addition, when you have that many people coming to church in one

175

city, you will see the city changed! The gifts of the Spirit do have a work in saving cities.

The gifts bring help to individuals, but do not limit the gifts to just that. Let them have full course in your ministry. Flow with them and move with them, because they also can be weapons of our warfare.

Spiritual warfare is an expression of God's love. Changing the voices of cities is an expression and an activity of God's love. Jesus is moved with compassion over the multitudes in cities, just as He was when He walked on earth.

> And Jesus went about all the cities and villages, teaching in their synagogues, and preaching the gospel of the kingdom, and healing every sickness and every disease among the people. But when he saw the multitudes, he was *moved with compassion* on them, because they fainted, and were scattered abroad, as sheep having no shepherd. Then saith he unto his disciples, The harvest truly is plenteous, but the labourers are few; pray ye therefore the Lord of the harvest, that he will send forth labourers into his harvest (Matt. 9:35-38, italics added).

Jesus is moved today by the plight of the multitudes, and He is saying to His church: "Reap the spiritual fruit of those cities."

The cry of Jesus is to reap souls. That will change the voice of that city.

There are several phases to God's operations in cities. There is the reaping of souls, and there is the fulfilling of His plan for that place. Souls were reaped in Jerusalem in Jesus' day, but God's plan for the city was not fulfilled. Let us do all we can to see that His plan for our cities has every chance at fulfillment.

Jesus worked at doing the Father's will, and it was not His fault that the city did not change. We need to work just as hard to see that we are not in any way accountable if our cities refuse Jesus.

Do Not Let It Die

The last thing to consider is this: Once the voice of the city changes, do not let the work die. You cannot sit down and "rest on your laurels." Keep praying and doing warfare to maintain the victory.

People tend to be one-sided in their approach to evangelism. They go after souls — and that is very important — but then they do not occupy the territory from which those souls come. The result, quite often, is the loss of souls once won.

Keep Praying — Keep Advancing

John Wesley once said that he did not believe God did anything unless people prayed.

This is the key to taking our cities and changing their voices. Spiritual warfare in prayer causes things to change. God is sovereign, but His sovereign will is to have His people be ambassadors on this earth, representing Him. In the Old Testament, Israel was to represent God to the nonbelievers (the Gentiles), and they were to speak forth His Word through prophetic utterances and through prayer (Is. 42:6, 49:6, 66:19).

177

Today that is our job. We're seeing it happen. Look what has happened in Eastern Europe. Much prayer went forth in Europe from God's oppressed people there. Before anything started to change in the natural order of things, however, the Spirit of the Lord was speaking it forth through prophecy. The Lord has spoken concerning other walls in the world as well.

The following prophecy came forth in one of my meetings.

> Yes, the wall in East Germany has fallen, but there are other walls throughout the world that shall fall, too. The walls that are built in the Middle East — they, too, shall tumble and fall. You will begin to see changes in the climate of the Middle East, for I will also have a harvest there. I *will* have My will performed there.
>
> So there has come a change in the realm of the Holy Spirit over the Middle East nations. It will look one way in the natural, but it is going to be changing to fit the changes of the Spirit. For the walls in that part of the world have flaunted themselves too long against My people, and they have decreed things against My people.
>
> And the evil princes [Dan. 10:13] have labored and warred against My move and My people. And now I shall go into battle there, and again the Middle East shall know that I am the God of the world and that I own the nations and that it is *My* will that shall be performed.

There are changes in that part of the world, and there will be those who receive a burden, a divine calling, to the nations of the Middle East. And those callings are not to be worried about but to be taken in, rejoiced over and prayed through. Then shall come the "walking out" [of these things]. And it will come very fast, for the Middle East *shall* change. For there is a harvest in those nations.

There will come great churches there that have been held down for many years, and they will carry great weight and governmental power in the Spirit. The Middle East shall know My name and My glory. My church shall grow strong there, as it will not be underground, but it will be public and bold. You ask how. There will come great miracles and great interventions, and you will know that when these things be, it was done by My miraculous hands.

So don't worry, you that are from those lands. I have not forgotten you, but I have heard your cry and come to answer you. I have come to answer your prayers, even your sorrows I have heard. You will see in the natural what I have shown you by the Spirit. Yes, says the Spirit of God, I am going to move.

For several months before that meeting I had been carrying the Middle East on my heart. I knew a special impartation was coming for the Middle East. In the late 1980s a couple — medical doctors in the nation of Oman — came to my office.

"You are supposed to come to Oman," they said.

At the time I thought that was an island off the African continent. I did not know Middle Eastern geography very well.

"Well, I don't know if I want to go," I said. "I'll send my books, but you know I have to *know* that God wants me to go."

But they kept begging me to come. It was not an asking from the soul but an urgent begging from their hearts. So I prayed and looked up Oman on the map. I sensed a divine begging coming out of those countries, just as Macedonia called for help from the apostle Paul.

> And a vision appeared to Paul in the night; There stood a man of Macedonia, and prayed him, saying, Come over into Macedonia, and help us.
>
> And after he had seen the vision, immediately we endeavoured to go into Macedonia, assuredly gathering that the Lord had called us for to preach the gospel unto them (Acts 16:9-10).

For the next few days after that couple visited me, the Spirit of God kept coming to me at intervals. "Go for two weeks," He would say.

Finally I said, "Two weeks? That's all? All right, I'll go."

I figured I could handle any place for two weeks. But I had to reach out for joy to make the trip because I had heard all these wild stories about the Middle East. But the Lord said go, so I went.

We took some books and teaching tapes that had

been translated into Arabic. We got them through the border without any trouble, which was a miracle. When I got into the country — you talk about warfare! Forget about sleeping. It's called "Pray to stay alive. Pray to stay in the will of God." I would lie in bed at night and just groan in my spirit in order to be able to breathe right. That is how dense the spiritual atmosphere there was.

We began the meetings, and people came. Hundreds came, and each day I noticed that the couple who had originally invited me there kept getting happier and happier. All during the meetings, this woman's smile kept getting wider and wider.

As the week went on, a lot of spiritual warfare was necessary. We broke through the spiritual resistance, and the last night of the meeting, the rejoicing of the Lord came. Those Christians danced in the church. They raised their hands and began to pray and dance in the Spirit.

Now to most charismatics in the United States, that may not sound very revolutionary. But for churches in that part of the world, it's a major spiritual breakthrough.

One night toward the end of that first week, as the doctor took me back to where I was staying, the wife said to me, "Roberts, you don't know what happened tonight. The vision I saw has happened. It's been accomplished. When I looked at the people tonight and saw their faces and what they were doing, it was exactly as I had seen it and called it."

"What vision?" I asked her. She hadn't told me about any vision.

So then she told me she had seen in her spirit that a time would come in Oman when the people in the church would have liberty in the Spirit. She saw them strong in the movings of the Holy Spirit and not bound and oppressed. She saw them singing and dancing and praising God with uplifted hands.

What she saw came to pass. She was really excited, but then she told me, "But in the midst of the rejoicing, I saw the next step. I am so happy for what has happened, but now I have something else for which to believe."

She had been given another goal in the task of changing the voice of her city and nation. She was determined to keep advancing. Later she told me about all the struggles of faith they'd been through, but she just kept believing ruthlessly that what she saw in her spirit would manifest. And it did.

This couple — the wife, in particular — was responsible for changing the climate of that city. They knew their responsibility and carried it out.

God has not forgotten the Middle East. He has not forgotten the Christians there. He has not forgotten that His words which have been spoken over those nations will be performed.

We can change our cities for God, In the days ahead we shall see many cities and nations changed. I want to be part of it, don't you?

I want to point out that I am not talking about taking over the natural governments of the world. We are not in competition with them. God's purpose is not to take them over but to change them into the likeness of His dear Son. That is done in the spiritual realm, not the natural arena.

When the spiritual powers over a city are changed, however, it will manifest or be reflected in the natural realm. That's what happened in the

Welsh Revival. When the move of God swept the nation of Wales, it not only brought souls into the body of Christ, but it also transformed whole towns and villages. Bars closed; mining operations were run differently; churches exploded. Things changed in the natural as a result of the spiritual changes.

A cry of righteousness went up from the entire nation, and the nation was changed. The sad thing was that it did not remain changed. People let go of what was happening. Once the revival was over, Christians decreased their efforts. The battle was won, but they needed to increase their efforts in order to hold the ground they had gained.

In these days before us, we are not going to let go and slacken up. The church is going to be made up of wise warriors. We are going to secure what we have taken hold of in the Spirit. We are going to have the cities of the world.

This is our destiny.

12

OUR FINAL DESTINY

The disciples came to Jesus asking, "Tell us, when shall these things be? and what shall be the sign of thy coming, and of the end of the world?"

Matthew 24:3

THE DISCIPLES knew that at some time in the future the world would come to an end. Naturally they were apprehensive about that. Who wouldn't be? In the natural, Jesus' reply was quite frightening. But spiritually it's exciting. Jesus told them:

Take heed that no man deceive you. For many shall come in my name, saying, I am Christ; and shall deceive many.

And ye shall hear of wars and rumours of wars: see that ye be not troubled: for all these things must come to pass, but the end is not yet.

For nation shall rise against nation, and kingdom against kingdom: and there shall be famines, and pestilences, and earthquakes, in divers places. All these are the beginning of sorrows.

Then shall they deliver you up to be afflicted, and shall kill you: and ye shall be hated of all nations for my name's sake. And then shall many be offended, and shall betray one another, and shall hate one another.

And many false prophets shall rise, and shall deceive many. And because iniquity shall abound, the love of many shall wax cold (Matt. 24:4-12)

This passage of Scripture paints a pretty bleak picture of the future before us. Fortunately, Jesus didn't stop there. He went on to say:

But he that shall endure unto the end, the same shall be saved. And this gospel of the kingdom shall be preached in all the world for a witness unto all nations; and then shall the end come (Matt. 24:13-14).

Now that's good news that we can grab hold of and run with. We can and will endure to the end.

We must, for we are the final witness unto all nations. That is our end-times role in the days ahead.

Completing His Work

As we read the Bible and study church history, we see how different men and women of God were used mightily for very specific purposes for their time. Abraham fulfilled his purpose on earth having received the covenant promise from God and fathering Isaac, from whom came the nation of Israel. Noah fulfilled his purpose in building the ark. Esther fulfilled her purpose in saving her entire people from annihilation. David fulfilled his purpose in killing Goliath and reigning as king. Joseph and Mary fulfilled their purpose in parenting Jesus. John the Baptist fulfilled his purpose in being Jesus' forerunner.

As you can see, each had a specific purpose for being here. So do we. Oh, that we would totally and completely fulfill God's purpose for our being here.

Jesus stood before the Father and said, "I have glorified thee on the earth: I have finished the work which thou gavest me to do" (John 17:4).

Jesus fulfilled the reason He was here. Now it's up to us to fulfill our time and reason for being here. We must stay on the cutting edge of life in the Spirit to endure until the end and be the strong, bold witnesses that God created us to be. That is our final destiny. That is why we are here on this earth today.

Have you ever asked yourself, Why am I here? What's the purpose for my being alive at this time in history?

I think at one time or another we all ask those

questions. When I was a little boy, I remember watching Westerns, and I'd imagine what it must have been like to live back in those days. Sometimes I'd even wish that I could have been alive then to experience what it was like to tame the West and conquer new territories.

Now I realize that although those may have been exciting times in the natural, today we are living in a much more exciting time in the spiritual realm. We are the generation that is responsible for the final approach to the end!

It's an awesome responsibility, but we shouldn't let it weigh us down. We should rise up rejoicing that God chose us to be part of the final days before His coming.

We all have a place in the body of Christ. Some are called to preach or teach. Some are called to start new churches. Some are called to be missionaries. Others lead praise and worship or work with children or youth. All that is important, but the most important reason we are here is that we are all called to be a final witness to this world.

That is our ultimate call — each and every one of us. To each of us God has given the ministry of reconciliation. All believers are His ambassadors.

Challenges Ahead

The time before us will be challenging. But with the challenge come the strength and faith to accomplish our high calling. David has gone before us to teach us that "the battle is the Lord's" (1 Sam. 17:47).

Just as God gave the giant into David's hands, He will give the nations into our hands. But the giant didn't just fall into David's hands. David had his part to play. Notice what he did.

When David faced the enemy, he *ran* toward him (1 Sam. 17:48). With total confidence for victory, David *ran* straight at the enemy. That took guts!

The more David talked about God in the face of his foe, the more strength and faith he produced within himself to get the job done.

We have a great job before us — preaching the good news in all the nations of the world before the end comes. God has given us everything we need to get the job done victoriously, just as He provided David with everything he needed to accomplish his task. All it took for David was one little stone to fell his enemy.

Whatever it takes to get the gospel to the nations, God will make sure we can do it. But it's up to us to go. It's up to us to obey and fulfill our destiny.

It has been said, "Do what you can with what you have where you are." I like that. We can all do something. And if we all do the something that God puts in us to do, the nations will be won by our witness during the final approach.

Claiming New Territories

Claiming new territories for God is where it's at today. We hear so much about thrill seekers. There are those who skydive, kayak or repel down towering mountain faces. Most recently, bungee jumping has become the new thrill.

I once asked a skydiver, "Why do you do it?" As far as I'm concerned, the last thing I would want to do is jump out of an airplane at five thousand feet, so I figured there must be some good reason why people do it.

The answer was, "I love the thrill. There's no other rush like it."

Well, that's fine if that's what makes you happy, I guess. But I have found that natural thrills are nothing in comparison to the thrill of fulfilling God's plan and purpose on this earth. That's what real fun is all about.

If you crave adventure with God and hunger to make a lasting impact on this earth for His glory, then you are alive at the right time. You are one of those final witnesses that Jesus spoke of — one of the final witnesses that the world is so in need of.

It is time for a strong, bold generation to rise up and bring revival to the nations. That is why we are here at this time in history. I no longer look back to the old days and wish I had lived in another time. I rejoice that I'm alive today. I am honored that God would choose me to live in this time of history.

It's the most exciting, thrilling time to be alive. The great patriarchs who are waiting for us in heaven would probably "give their eye teeth" to be able to live in this time. They went before us and paved the way. The rest is up to us. I don't want to let them down, do you? But most important, I don't want to let down my Lord and King.

Our generation is responsible to reach this world for Jesus Christ. I am fully committed to that. My hope in writing this book was to impart that desire to you — that you would commit yourself fully to being the final witness that you are called to be, that you will reach this world for Christ in the church's final approach to eternity. I pray that your high calling comes forth in great boldness and strength so you can go forth to be a mighty blessing to the nations.

Dare to go where God is leading you. Dare to do what He is calling you to do. He won't ever let you down. There's a great big world out there waiting for YOU...God's final witness. You can do it.

NOTES

Chapter Six

1. James Strong, *The New Strong's Exhaustive Concordance of the Bible* (Nashville: Thomas Nelson Publishers, 1984). See the Hebrew and Chaldee dictionary, #5459, p. 82.

2. *Ibid.* See the Greek dictionary of the New Testament, #4041, p. 57.

If you enjoyed *Final Approach*, we would like
to recommend the following books:

Prophetic Destinies
by Derek Prince
How does the church relate to the Jews and
the state of Israel? Author Derek Prince answers
that question based on a lifetime of study and
experience. You will discover how the prophetic
destinies of Israel and the church are intertwined.

Thinking the Unthinkable
by John Wesley White
Author John Wesley White shows how Old and New
Testament prophecies mesh remarkably with comments from
dozens of experts in politics, science and economics. He
masterfully traces God's agenda for the future and shows you
how to find personal peace in these turbulent times.

Revelation
by Paul Yonggi Cho
Paul Yonggi Cho is pastor of the world's largest church,
the Full Gospel Church in Seoul, Korea. In his book *Revelation*
he unlocks the mystery behind the symbolism of this difficult
yet fascinating book of the Bible. He relates past and present
world events to the words recorded by the apostle John.

Available at your local Christian bookstore or from:

Creation House
600 Rinehart Road
Lake Mary, FL 32746
1-800-451-4598